THE *Pioneer Woman Cooks*

FOOD FROM MY FRONTIER

THE

Pioneer Woman Cooks

Food

FROM MY
FRONTIER

REE DRUMMOND

WM

WILLIAM MORROW
An Imprint of HarperCollinsPublishers

All photographs by Ree Drummond except the following: title page and pages 3 and 124 by Shane Bevel; dedication page courtesy of Ga-Ga; page 16 by Marlboro Man.

HarperCollins books may be purchased for educational, business, or sales promotional use. For information please write: Special Markets Department, HarperCollins Publishers, 10 East 53rd Street, New York, NY 10022.

FIRST EDITION

Designed by Kris Tobiassen

Library of Congress Cataloging-in-Publication Data has been applied for.
ISBN 978-0-06-199718-1

15 16 17 RRD 20 19 18 17

For Ga-Ga

CONTENTS

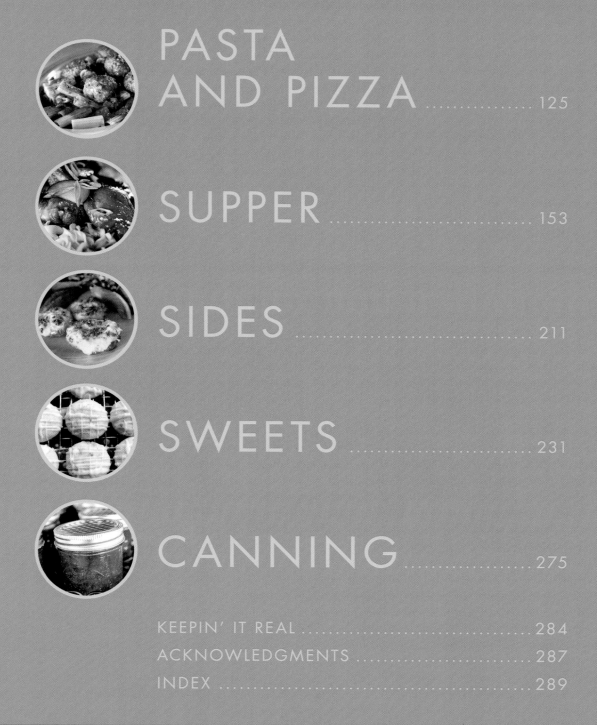

Also by Ree Drummond

The Pioneer Woman Cooks: Recipes from an Accidental Country Girl

The Pioneer Woman: Black Heels to Tractor Wheels—A Love Story

Charlie the Ranch Dog

THE

Pioneer Woman Cooks

FOOD FROM MY FRONTIER

INTRODUCTION
Oh, Give Me Food, Lots of Food...

That's the chorus I sang over and over in my head as I cooked, tested, photographed, and wrote this, my second cookbook, over a period of many, many months. When I began, I knew I wanted to take a slightly different approach than I had with my first cookbook, which will always be my first love. Where my first one offered hearty family recipes interspersed with photos and stories from the country, I wanted this baby to be filled to the brim with food, food, and food galore—along with all the step-by-step photographs I've always loved to share. Where my first book really delivered on the cows, kids, and canine companions, I wanted this one to deliver on the suppers, sides, and sweets.

Of course, I couldn't help but share all the things I love about my life in the country.

You'll still see the dogs . . .

and the horses . . .

and the kids . . .

and the scenery.

But most of all, you'll see food. Glorious, abundant, mouthwatering, crowd-pleasing food.

Some recipes in this book are old classics from my website, many of them recooked, retested, and rephotographed to ensure as much visual lusciousness and guaranteed deliciousness as possible. But I'm also including a good crop of new recipes I've never shared before—all guaranteed to win friends, influence people, garner marriage proposals, foster friendships, mend fences, and make you the most popular person in town.

(Or at least in your family.)

(Which is really all that matters anyway.)

Lots of Love,

Pioneer Woman

BREAKFAST

PERFECT ICED COFFEE

Makes approximately 1½ gallons iced coffee concentrate

Iced coffee is my life. I've been an iced coffee freakazoid for years and years. To say I couldn't live without it is an understatement. It gives me the tools I need to cope.

Iced coffee is a complicated thing. One would think that one could merely pour brewed coffee into a glass full of ice and call it a day . . . but I find that method extremely flawed. No matter how packed with ice the glass is, once the hot coffee hits, some of the ice is bound to melt. This has two disastrous results:

1. The overall strength of the coffee flavor is diluted.

2. The iced coffee isn't as cold as it could (or should) be.

Lucky for me and my lucidity, I discovered the cold-brew method for creating iced coffee concentrate, which is much smoother and less acidic than traditionally brewed coffee. I've made iced coffee this way ever since, and can tell you that there is no better (or simpler) method for having the most delicious (and cheap!) iced coffee at your fingertips.

1 pound ground coffee (good, rich roast)
8 quarts cold water
Milk or half-and-half (a healthy splash per serving)
Sweetened condensed milk (2 to 3 tablespoons per serving)

1. Place the ground coffee into a large container.

2. Pour in 8 quarts cold water.

3. Give it a stir to make sure all the grounds are wet.

4. Then place the lid on the container and let it sit on the counter at room temperature for 12 to 24 hours.

5. Lay some cheesecloth in a fine-mesh strainer. Slowly pour the coffee/water mixture through the strainer and into a clean container or vat.

6. At the end, gently press the grounds with a spoon to make sure all the liquid makes it through. Discard the cheesecloth with the grounds inside. It's a royal mess, dude.

7. Place the vat in the refrigerator and allow the coffee concentrate to cool.

8. To serve the coffee, dispense the concentrate into a glass filled with ice.

9. Splash in milk or half-and-half . . .

10. And some sweetened condensed milk.

11. Listen. Do you hear that? It's calling out your name.

12. Stir it to mix and enjoy it immediately.

Repeat daily as needed. I sure do.

Variation

You may use skim milk, 2%, whole milk, sugar, artificial sweeteners, syrups—adapt to your liking.

Sinful Variation

Mix coffee concentrate with vanilla ice cream and blend. Coffee milkshake!

HOMEMADE GLAZED DOUGHNUTS

Makes about 24 doughnuts

These take a little patience . . . but boy oh boy, are they worth it. Make the dough the night before so you can have fresh, warm doughnuts in the morning.

And you'll live happily ever after.

Please be careful when cooking with hot oil.

DOUGHNUTS

¼ cup granulated sugar

1⅛ cups whole milk, very warm

3 teaspoons instant yeast

2 large eggs

1¼ sticks unsalted butter, melted

4 cups all-purpose flour

¼ teaspoon salt

4 cups vegetable shortening, for frying (or peanut or safflower oil)

GLAZE

3 cups powdered sugar

½ teaspoon salt

½ teaspoon vanilla extract

½ cup cold water

1. In a medium bowl, add the granulated sugar to the warm milk.

2. Then add the yeast. Allow it to sit for 5 to 10 minutes, or until the yeast is starting to bubble.

3. In a small bowl, beat the eggs.

4. Then pour them into a bowl with the melted butter, whisking constantly.

5. Add the butter/egg mixture to the bowl of an electric mixer. Pour in the milk/sugar/yeast mixture.

6. With the hook attachment, turn the mixer to low speed.

7. Mix the flour and salt in a bowl, then retrieve ½ cup at a time . . .

8. And add it to the mixing bowl, allowing it to slowly incorporate into the liquid mixture.

9. Continue mixing for 5 minutes after the flour is combined. Stop the mixer, scrape the bowl, and mix for 30 seconds more. Then place the dough in a lightly oiled bowl, cover it with plastic wrap, and refrigerate it for 8 to 12 hours.

10. The next morning, remove the dough from the fridge and allow it to come to room temperature and rise for 1½ to 2 hours. Put it in a warm spot if necessary to facilitate rising.

11. Turn it out onto a floured surface . . .

12. And roll it out to about ¼ inch thick.

13. Use a doughnut cutter (or two concentric biscuit cutters) to cut out the doughnuts.

14. Did I just use the word *concentric* correctly? I sure hope so.

15. Remove the holes and transfer the doughnuts to a lightly floured baking sheet lined with a baking mat or parchment. Then—and this is the vital part—cover lightly with tea towels and place it in a draft-free area of your kitchen for at least 1½ to 2 hours.

16. It'll take that long for them to do this. Light as a feather! (If they don't seem to be rising much, move the pan to a warm place.)

17. Melt the shortening in a pot over medium-high heat till it reaches 350°F on a candy thermometer. (Or you can drop one of the doughnut holes into the oil. If it sizzles and immediately rises to the surface, the oil is ready.) Carefully drop the doughnuts, a few at a time, into the oil.

18. They should immediately float to the top and puff up.

19. Then use a metal spoon or spatula to carefully flip them over to the other side.

20. Remove them from the oil as soon as they're golden brown on both sides (this should take less than a minute total).

21. At the end, drop in the doughnut holes and fry them until they're golden brown.

22. Place the doughnuts on paper towel–lined plates to drain. Don't worry if they're a little imperfect; if your fingers leave impressions when you dropped them into the oil, that just means they were extra light and fluffy.

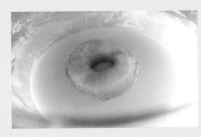

23. To glaze the doughnuts, mix the powdered sugar, salt, vanilla, and water in a bowl until smooth. Drop in the doughnuts one at a time.

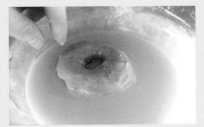

24. Quickly turn them over.

25. Then remove them . . .

26. And place them on a rack so that the excess glaze can drip off.

27. To make the most of the glaze, set the holes underneath the doughnuts so they can catch the extra good stuff.

28. Then stick 'em in a basket or box and deliver them to a doughnut-head in your life.

Variation

Replace the vanilla extract with a splash of orange or maple extract to give the glaze a slightly different flavor.

Our house. In the middle of our ranch.

MAKE-AHEAD MUFFIN MELTS

Makes 12 muffin melts

I love this breakfast treat because you can make the spread ahead of time, keep it in the fridge, then just spread it on English muffins and broil them as the A.M. appetites in your house dictate.

12 slices bacon

12 hard-boiled eggs, peeled and chopped

2 cups grated Cheddar cheese

1 cup (real) mayonnaise

1 heaping tablespoon Dijon mustard, or more to taste

½ teaspoon garlic powder

5 dashes of Worcestershire sauce

6 English muffins, split

1. Fry the bacon until chewy and slightly crisp.

2. Use a knife to chop it up, then put it somewhere safe so your family won't wolf it down like mine does. Please feel sorry for me.

3. Peel the hard-boiled eggs.

4. Then give 'em a rough chop.

5. Add the cheese, the chopped bacon, and the mayonnaise to a bowl.

6. Next, add some Dijon mustard . . .

7. Along with the garlic powder and Worcestershire sauce.

8. Fold all the ingredients together, then give it a taste. Add more of whatever you think it needs!

9. Preheat your oven's broiler to low.

10. Spread a good amount of the spread on the halved English muffins.

11. Place them on the lower rack of the oven and broil them for 3 to 4 minutes, being careful not to burn them. The topping should be hot and the cheese should be melted.

Yummy . . .

For my tummy!

You have to make these to believe how good they are.

Variations

- *Stir finely diced onion and/or bell pepper into the egg/cheese mixture.*

- *Use Pepper Jack cheese instead of Cheddar for a little kick.*

- *Toast on a bagel half instead of an English muffin.*

- *Spread on sandwich bread and add lettuce and tomato for a twist on egg salad.*

ORANGE SWEET ROLLS

Makes approximately 48 rolls

These wonderfully sticky and sweet breakfast rolls are my favorite variation on my mother's world-famous cinnamon rolls, which I deliver to friends every Christmas as part of a lifelong tradition. While the originals will always hold a special place in my heart, this orange version—made extra special and interesting with the tangy bittersweetness of marmalade—runs a very, very close second.

Try to eat just one of them. I double dog dare ya.

DOUGH

2 cups whole milk

½ cup granulated sugar

½ cup vegetable oil

2¼ teaspoons active dry yeast

4½ cups all-purpose flour

½ rounded teaspoon baking powder

½ rounded teaspoon baking soda

2 teaspoons salt

FILLING

½ cup (1 stick) butter, melted

8 tablespoons orange marmalade

1 cup lightly packed brown sugar

¼ teaspoon salt

ICING

Zest and juice of 2 oranges

1 cup powdered sugar

Dash of salt

½ cup whole milk, more if needed for a pourable consistency

4 tablespoons (½ stick) butter, melted

1. In a large saucepan over low heat, heat the milk, granulated sugar, and oil until warm but not hot. Add the yeast and 4 cups of flour, then mix and transfer to a bowl. Cover and let it rise for at least an hour.

2. Stir in the remaining ½ cup flour, the baking powder, baking soda, and salt.

3. Roll the dough into a long rectangle, about 30 inches wide by 10 inches deep. You'll want it to be as thin as you can get it so that you can add plenty of goo.

4. Drizzle the melted butter all over the surface of the dough. Use your fingers to smear it all around so that it coats evenly.

5. Spread the orange marmalade all over the buttered dough, distributing it as evenly as you can.

6. Sprinkle plenty of brown sugar all over the marmalade . . .

7. And finish with a light sprinkling of salt to offset the sweetness.

8. Using both hands in a back-and-forth motion, gradually roll the dough toward you into one long log.

9. Pinch the seam to seal it.

10. Then slice the log-o'-dough into ½-inch pieces.

11. Preheat the oven to 375°F. Place the rolls in a buttered baking dish and allow them to rise for 20 minutes. Bake for 15 to 17 minutes.

12. While the rolls are baking, make the icing: Add the zest and juice of 2 oranges to a bowl.

15. And some more melted butter because the recipe doesn't already have enough. Just kidding on that last part.

17. Pull the rolls out of the oven when they're golden brown and drizzle on the icing right off the bat.

13. Add the powdered sugar and salt . . .

16. Whisk it together until it's nice and smooth and lovely. Your kitchen smells like oranges! Unless you're making this in the garage. In that case, your garage smells like oranges.

18. The piping hot rolls will suck that gorgeous icing right down into their crevices and the whole thing pretty much becomes a miracle.

Serve them warm.

14. Some whole milk . . .

Pop Quiz: Is this 6:00 am or 6:00 pm?

EGGS BENEDICT

Makes 4 servings

Eggs Benedict holds the distinction of being on the select list of recipes I'd choose to eat on the last day of my life or the day after the last day of my diet . . . whichever comes first.

　　I realize that made absolutely no sense. Hollandaise sauce has that effect on me.

3 egg yolks

Juice of 2 lemons

2 sticks butter, melted and slightly cooled

Dash of salt

Cayenne pepper to taste

4 eggs

2 English muffins, split, buttered, and toasted

4 slices Canadian bacon, warmed in a skillet

Dash of paprika

1. Add the egg yolks to a blender or food processor.

2. Add the lemon juice.

3. Blend for several seconds.

4. With the blender on, slowly drizzle in the melted butter.

5. Peek through the hole in the blender lid. Get excited. Very good things are happening in there.

6. Turn off the blender and add a little salt and cayenne. Whip it again until combined. Set this aside for a minute.

7. Next, poach an egg by gently cracking an egg into simmering, slightly bubbling water. Leave the egg alone for 1½ to 2 minutes, or until the yolk is still slightly soft/runny, then remove it with a slotted spoon and carefully place it on a plate. Repeat with the remaining eggs.

8. To serve, place a buttered, toasted English muffin half on a plate.

9. Top the English muffin with a warm slice of Canadian bacon.

10. Place the warm poached egg on top. And then . . . get ready to be really, really happy.

11. Drizzle on the warm hollandaise.

12. Sprinkle a little paprika on top so it'll look extra purty.

This is absolute perfection. I'm so glad I finished my diet yesterday.

EGGS FLORENTINE

Makes 4 servings

This is a delicious variation of Eggs Benedict that uses wilted spinach in place of Canadian bacon. Perfect for vegans! Well . . . except for the whole egg thing.

And the whole butter thing.

Never mind.

8 ounces baby spinach

1 tablespoon butter

1. Sauté the spinach in the butter in a medium skillet over medium-high heat. A minute later, remove the spinach from the heat. Arrange the spinach on top of a buttered, toasted English muffin.

3. And drizzle on the hollandaise! This is always my favorite part.

2. Place a poached egg on top of the spinach.

4. Wait. I changed my mind. *This* is always my favorite part.

5. Sprinkle a little paprika on top at the end. Yum!

Morning: The most wonderful (yawwwwwwwwn . . .
grooooooan . . . where's my coffee?) time of day.

LEMON BLUEBERRY PANCAKES

Makes 4 servings

I decided to make these pancakes one day because I had an open can of leftover evaporated milk. Oh, and because I wanted pancakes . . . but that's nothing new. I threw some lemon juice and zest into the evaporated milk for two reasons. One: The juice, when combined with the evaporated milk, results in a little bit of a buttermilk effect. Two: I love lemon and blueberries together. Three: I love Ethel Merman.

(Don't pay any attention to me, okay? It only encourages me.)

Zest and juice of 1 lemon
(and more juice if needed)

1½ cups evaporated milk
(more if needed)

1½ cups plus 1 tablespoon
cake flour

¼ teaspoon salt

1 heaping tablespoon baking
powder

3 tablespoons sugar

1 large egg

1½ teaspoons vanilla extract

1 heaping cup blueberries

2 tablespoons butter, melted, plus
extra butter for serving

Warmed pure maple or pancake
syrup, for serving

1. Zest the lemon and set the zest aside. Squeeze the lemon juice into the evaporated milk. Stir and let it sit for a few minutes to thicken.

2. In a large bowl, combine the cake flour and salt. Best added with a freaky pink alien claw like the one you see above.

Take me to your leader.

3. Add the baking powder and sugar—you'll need plenty to offset the tartness of all that lemon! (Sorry to shout!)

6. Add the wet mixture to the dry ingredients, stirring it gently with a fork as you pour it in. Be careful not to overmix it.

9. Heat a heavy griddle or skillet over medium-low heat and add 2 tablespoons of butter to the pan. Use a ¼ cup measure to drop the batter into the pan.

4. Crack an egg into the evaporated milk/lemon mixture and add the vanilla, which is my weapon of choice with any pancake recipe.

7. Then fold in a whole bunch o' blueberries. Splash in a little more evaporated milk if it's overly thick. It needs to be slightly pourable, not just ploppable.

10. Then cook 'em on both sides until golden brown.

5. Add the lemon zest to the evaporated milk mixture and stir to combine. Smell that yummy citrus!

8. Finally, stir in the melted butter.

11. Stack 'em up to your heart's content, top with a big pat of softened butter, drizzle on the warm syrup, and enjoy!

I believe I can . . . fly?

Variation

Substitute real buttermilk for the evaporated milk/lemon juice mixture and omit the lemon zest for traditional blueberry pancakes.

BREAKFAST BREAD PUDDING

Makes 8 to 10 servings

Make this breakfast casserole the night before and store it, unbaked, in the fridge. Then just pop it in the oven when you get out of bed the next morning. Hearty and divine!

1 large yellow onion, thinly sliced

3 tablespoons butter

1 pound breakfast sausage

8 slices Texas toast (or other thick-sliced bread), lightly toasted and set aside to dry for a few hours

1 red bell pepper, chopped

2 cups grated Monterey Jack cheese

8 eggs

¾ cup half-and-half

Salt and black pepper to taste

Dash of cayenne pepper (optional)

1. In a large skillet over medium heat, sauté the onion in 2 tablespoons of the butter until golden brown, about 10 minutes. Remove to a plate.

2. Brown and crumble the breakfast sausage in the same skillet. Set aside.

3. Use the remaining 1 tablespoon of butter to grease a 2-quart baking dish. Tear the Texas toast into chunks and and lay half of them in the dish.

7. Repeat the layers, ending with the cheese and arranging a few chunks of the crust so they stick out of the top.

11. Bake, still covered in foil, for 20 minutes, then remove the foil and bake for 10 to 15 minutes more, or until the top is golden brown.

4. Add half the crumbled sausage . . .

8. Lightly beat together the eggs and half-and-half. Stir in salt and pepper to taste and a bit of cayenne, if you want a little heat. Pour the egg mixture over the top.

5. Half the onions . . .

12. Dish it up and serve immediately.

Variations

- *Substitute crumbled bacon or diced ham for the sausage.*

- *Use crusty French bread or ciabatta bread instead of Texas toast.*

- *Substitute Cheddar or Swiss for the Monterey Jack.*

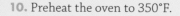

9. Cover the dish with aluminum foil and place it in the fridge for several hours or overnight.

10. Preheat the oven to 350°F.

6. Half the red pepper, and half the cheese.

BREAKFAST PIZZA

Makes 8 to 10 servings

Hash browns? Diced peppers? Bacon? Fried eggs? On . . . on *pizza*?

You'd better believe it, baby. This is a satisfying and ultra-hearty pizza for hungry mornings in your house. Crack on as many eggs as you need!

1 pound thick-cut peppered bacon

3 cups frozen hash browns

2 tablespoons vegetable oil

1 red bell pepper, diced

1 green bell pepper, diced

1 yellow bell pepper, diced

Pizza Dough (page 141)

½ cup salsa, plus more for serving (page 92, or your favorite store-bought variety)

12 ounces fresh mozzarella, sliced

8 large eggs

Salt and black pepper to taste

1. Preheat the oven to 475°F. Place the oven rack in the lowest position.

2. Fry the bacon until chewy, then chop it into bite-size pieces.

3. Fry the frozen hash browns in a large skillet over medium-high heat with 1 tablespoon of the vegetable oil until they're just starting to turn golden brown. Remove from the pan and set them aside on a plate.

4. In the same skillet, fry the red, green, and yellow bell peppers over medium-high heat in the remaining 1 tablespoon vegetable oil for about 5 minutes, or until nice and brown. Set aside.

5. Roll out the pizza dough on a lightly oiled baking sheet. Spread the salsa all over the surface.

6. Evenly distribute the sliced mozzarella over the top.

7. Sprinkle on the hash browns . . .

8. The fried bell peppers . . .

9. And the bacon.

10. Next comes the fun part! Crack the eggs here and there all over the surface of the pizza. Be careful not to break the yolk or you'll have seven years of bad luck! (Or . . . wait. That's a broken mirror. Never mind.) Finally, sprinkle on salt and pepper to taste.

11. Bake for 13 to 15 minutes, or until the crust is golden brown and the eggs are set but still slightly soft. Cut into large pieces and serve immediately with extra salsa.

Variations

- *Substitute finely diced ham for the bacon.*
- *Serve with fresh pico de gallo or sour cream.*
- *Sprinkle the top with chopped cilantro.*

FRENCH TOAST WITH BERRY BUTTER

Makes 6 to 8 servings

This is how they serve French toast in Heaven. I heard a rumor.

1 pound (4 sticks) unsalted butter, softened, plus more for the skillet

¾ cup raspberries

¾ cup blackberries

4 eggs

2 cups half-and-half

1 tablespoon granulated sugar

2 teaspoons vanilla extract

Zest of 1 lemon

1 loaf crusty bread: baguette, French loaf, sourdough

Warmed pure maple syrup, for serving

Sifted powdered sugar, for serving (optional)

1. First, make the berry butter in 2 different batches: Whip ½ pound (2 sticks) of the butter until fluffy.

2. Add the raspberries . . .

3. Then switch to the paddle attachment and beat it on low speed for only a few rotations. The berries will break up immediately.

Pretty Kitty.

4. Lay a long sheet of plastic wrap on top of a long sheet of aluminum foil, then turn out the berry butter in a long (about 12 to 15 inches) log shape.

5. Carefully roll the butter inside the plastic wrap, then inside the foil. Twist the edges of the foil.

6. Continue twisting the edges in opposite directions to create pressure. This will force the butter into a uniform cylindrical shape. When you have it as tight as you can get it, place it in the fridge for several hours to firm up. (Or you can put it in the freezer to speed along the process.)

7. Repeat this process with the blackberries . . .

8. Then seal it up and store it in the fridge to harden.

9. Separate the eggs and store the whites for another use.

10. Pour the half-and-half into a large dish with the egg yolks and granulated sugar . . .

11. Then add the vanilla and lemon zest and whisk it together.

12. Throw in a couple of pieces of bread at a time, turning them over and allowing them to completely absorb the liquid.

13. Remove them from the dish and set them aside.

14. You can do small pieces, too!

15. When you're ready, melt plenty of butter in a skillet over medium heat, then cook the French toast until it's golden brown and slightly crisp.

16. Remove the berry butter from the fridge and unwrap the ends.

17. Slice off one of each variety . . .

18. And place them on each serving. Drizzle the top with warm maple syrup. Sift some powdered sugar on top if desired.

This is absolutely dreamy and very, very pretty.

Variations

- *Add ¼ cup powdered sugar to the mixer for a sweeter berry butter.*

- *Use blueberries or strawberries instead!*

- *Spread berry butter on muffins, croissants, toasted bagels, pancakes, and waffles.*

Cousins . . . Sisters . . . Friends!

COWBOY QUICHE

Makes one 10-inch quiche, to serve about 8

Quiche is, like, so 1979. But so is my taste in music. ("Heart of Glass," anyone?)

I've made this deep-dish quiche for years, and I'll make it till the day I croak. The filling is totally adaptable—throw in asparagus tips, broccoli, or whatever cheeses you have in your fridge. And if you're serving a crowd, the filling can be made ahead of time and stored in the fridge until you're ready to pour it into the crust and bake it.

This is the cowboy version. Ain't none of that weird stuff in it.

1 recipe Pam's Piecrust, enough for a deep pie dish (page 37)

8 slices bacon, fried until chewy

2 yellow onions, sliced

2 tablespoons butter

8 eggs

1½ cups heavy cream

Salt and black pepper to taste

2 cups grated sharp Cheddar cheese

1. Preheat the oven to 400°F.

2. Begin by rolling out the pie dough.

3. Gently lay it in a large tart or deep-dish pie pan . . .

4. And press it into the grooves in the pan. Set aside.

5. Chop up the bacon into bite-size pieces.

6. In a heavy skillet over medium-low heat, fry the onions in the butter until deep golden brown, 12 to 15 minutes.

7. Mix the eggs, cream, and salt and pepper in a bowl.

8. Add the bacon, onions, and cheese . . .

9. And stir to combine.

10. Pour the filling into the pie shell, cover lightly with aluminum foil, and bake for 45 minutes. Remove the foil and bake for an additional 10 minutes, or until the quiche is set and the crust is golden brown.

11. Remove from the oven and allow to sit for 10 minutes.

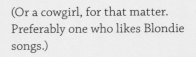

Fit for a king . . . or a cowboy.

(Or a cowgirl, for that matter. Preferably one who likes Blondie songs.)

Variation

Add 1 tablespoon finely diced jalapeño to the quiche mixture before baking for a spicy kick.

COWGIRL QUICHE

Makes one 10-inch quiche, to serve about 8

My cowgirl version of quiche is a little more girly . . . and every bit as delicious.

16 ounces white mushrooms, washed and sliced

2 leeks

2 tablespoons butter

8 eggs

1½ cups heavy cream

2 cups grated Swiss cheese

Salt and black pepper to taste

8 thin slices prosciutto (or any good ham)

1 recipe Pam's Piecrust (page 37), enough for a deep pie dish or tart pan

1. Preheat the oven to 400°F.

2. Place the mushrooms on a large baking sheet. Roast in the oven for 15 to 20 minutes, or until golden brown. Remove from the oven and set aside.

3. Meanwhile, lop off the tops and bottoms of the leeks and cut them in half lengthwise.

4. Slice each half thinly . . .

5. And soak the leeks in cold water for about 10 minutes to remove any grit or dirt.

6. In a large skillet over medium heat, sauté the leeks in the butter until golden brown and beginning to caramelize, 8 to 10 minutes. Set aside.

7. For the quiche base, add the eggs and cream to a medium bowl.

8. Whisk them to combine.

9. Stir in the leeks, mushrooms, grated cheese, salt and pepper . . .

10. And prosciutto.

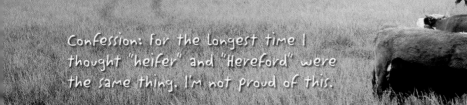

Confession: for the longest time I thought "heifer" and "Hereford" were the same thing. I'm not proud of this.

11. The mixture should be very thick!

13. Remove it from the oven and allow it to sit for at least 10 minutes before serving.

12. Pour it into the pie shell, then cover it loosely with a sheet of aluminum foil to prevent it from getting too brown on top. Bake for 45 minutes, then remove the foil and bake for an additional 10 minutes.

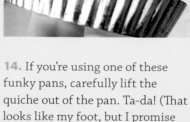

14. If you're using one of these funky pans, carefully lift the quiche out of the pan. Ta-da! (That looks like my foot, but I promise it isn't.)

15. Place it on a cutting board and slice wedges with a serrated knife.

Delicious for breakfast, even better for lunch with a salad and a bunch of juicy grapes.

Variation

Stir 2 tablespoons Pesto (page 137) into the quiche mixture before baking.

Gathering cattle on a warm summer morning. It's the stuff that dreams—and laundry rooms—were made of.

PAM'S PIECRUST

Makes one 9-inch, 2-crust pie

My good friend and fellow homeschooling mother Pam Regentin has a wedding cake business in Oregon called Fleur Cakes, but she's just as well known for her pies. Pam visited the ranch to teach a pie workshop once, and everyone fell madly in love with her crust.

    Butter was to blame.

2½ cups all-purpose or pastry flour

1 teaspoon salt

1 tablespoon sugar

1 cup (2 sticks) cold butter, cut into chunks

¼ cup cold water

1. Lightly mix 2 cups of the flour, the salt, and the sugar in a mixing bowl or in the bowl of a food processor.

2. Cut the butter into the flour using a pastry cutter or by pulsing the food processor. The mixture should look like large crumbs and begin to cling together in clumps. Add the remaining ½ cup flour and mix lightly or pulse the processor 2 or 3 times.

3. Do not overmix this flour. It should coat the clumps.

4. Sprinkle the cold water over the dough and with your hands or a wooden spoon, mix it in until the dough holds together, then shape the dough into 2 discs. At this point, you may wrap the dough in plastic wrap for storage; it will keep up to a week in the fridge or up to 6 months in the freezer.

5. Have ready 2 sheets of parchment paper that are each at least 12 inches square. Place 1 disc of dough between them. (If the dough is sticky for any reason, don't worry. Just sprinkle some flour on the parchment to get started. You shouldn't have to add much for it to stop sticking.) Starting at the center, roll the pin out to the edge. Turn the dough and parchment as necessary and continue rolling, always from the center to the outer edge. After a couple of rolls, lift the parchment paper away from the dough to loosen and replace the parchment. Flip the whole thing and loosen the other paper sheet. Continue rolling until the dough is large enough for your pie pan.

Use with Cowboy Quiche (page 32) and Cowgirl Quiche (page 34).

LUNCH

SPICY CAESAR SALAD

Makes 4 servings

I'm a Caesar salad lover. I'm also a chipotle pepper lover. I also happen to be a corn bread lover. Boy, do I get around!

This spicy variation on an old classic incorporates all my loves onto one great big happy plate. Serve it with soup for a yummy lunch, or serve it with grilled chicken or steaks as a scrumptious—and slightly different—side.

The dressing contains raw egg. While eggs are generally very safe, people who are very young, very old, or have a suppressed immune system should avoid eating them raw.

SALAD

2 garlic cloves, minced finely

1 tablespoon Dijon mustard

2 egg yolks

Juice of 1 lemon

1 teaspoon Worcestershire sauce

2 chipotle peppers in adobo sauce

¾ cup olive oil

Salt and black pepper to taste

1 recipe Cornbread Croutons (recipe follows)

¼ cup butter, melted

4 hearts of romaine lettuce, washed, dried, and separated

1. Add the minced garlic to a bowl.

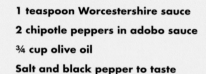

2. Throw in the Dijon.

3. Add the egg yolks . . .

4. And whisk to combine.

5. Squeeze in the lemon juice . . .

6. And add the Worcestershire sauce. So far, so good!

7. But now's when we depart from the norm. Grab a couple of canned chipotle peppers.

8. Mince them up finely, then add them to the dressing.

9. Whisk it all together, then begin drizzling in the olive oil in a thin stream, whisking constantly to emulsify.

10. Slowly but surely, it'll turn into a gorgeous, thick dressing. Add salt and pepper to taste. Cover the bowl and refrigerate it until you need it.

11. Toss the leaves gently in the Caesar dressing, or simply drizzle it over the leaves once they're on the plate.

12. Drop on plenty of croutons. They're delicious! If you have any left over, eat them as a snack . . . or sprinkle them over a bowl of beans.

Variation

Top with grilled chicken or shrimp for a main dish salad.

The face that launched a thousand sighs. From Mama.

CORNBREAD CROUTONS

3 tablespoons vegetable
shortening, melted

½ cup cornmeal (white or yellow)

¼ cup all-purpose flour

2 teaspoons baking powder

½ teaspoon salt

½ cup buttermilk (or ½ cup milk
mixed with ½ teaspoon white
vinegar)

¼ cup milk

1 small egg

¼ teaspoon baking soda

½ stick butter, melted

1. Preheat the oven to 400°F. Pour 1 tablespoon of the shortening into a medium-size iron skillet or a square 8 x 8-inch baking pan.

2. Combine the cornmeal, flour, baking powder, and salt in a mixing bowl. In a separate bowl, combine the buttermilk, milk, egg, and baking soda. Stir. Mix together the wet and dry ingredients until just combined, then stir in the remaining 2 tablespoons melted shortening. Pour into the skillet or baking pan, smoothing the surface with a knife or spatula. Bake for 15 to 20 minutes, or until golden brown on top.

4. Spread the cubes on a baking sheet and drizzle with the melted butter. Bake at 325°F, tossing or shaking occasionally, until the croutons are crisp, about 20 minutes. Allow the croutons to cool slightly before serving.

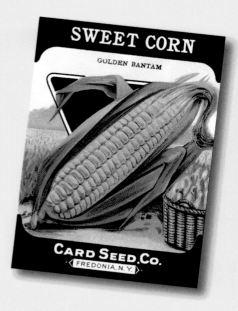

3. To make the croutons, cut the cornbread into 1-inch cubes.

Huh? What'd I ever do to you?

BEST GRILLED CHEESE EVER

Makes 4 servings

I first learned that grilled cheese sandwiches could be more than a just slice of cheese between two toast-ed pieces of bread at a sweet little lunch joint named Queenies. A mainstay in Tulsa, Oklahoma, Queenies serves heavenly soups, salads, and the best grilled cheese sandwiches you'll ever eat in your life.

Since Queenies isn't just around the corner from my house, I had to learn to make do on my own. Here's my version of one of their masterpieces.

I love you, Queenies! Please open a satellite location in our hay meadow. Thank you.

4 poblano or Anaheim chiles (or you may use canned whole green chiles)

¼ cup white vinegar

½ red onion, thinly sliced

¼ cup Dijon mustard

¼ cup mayonnaise

8 slices rye bread

12 slices provolone cheese

2 ripe tomatoes, thickly sliced

8 slices Cheddar cheese

½ cup (1 stick) butter, softened

1. Begin by roasting the chiles until the skin is blackened (if using fresh).

2. When the chiles are totally charred, throw them into a bowl.

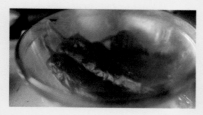

3. Cover them tightly with plastic wrap and let the peppers sit in the bowl and steam for a while.

4. Next, pour the white vinegar over the sliced red onion and let them sit awhile. This'll take away a little of the crazy onion flavor and leave them with a nice sweetness.

5. Finally, make the special sauce: equal amounts of mayonnaise and Dijon. It's the simple things in life!

6. When you're ready to make the sandwiches, scrape the blackened skin off of the chiles. Scrape out the seeds, too, so you'll wind up with big pieces of roasted green chiles.

7. For each sandwich, generously spread 2 pieces of rye bread (this is fancy, swirly pumpernickel rye) with the special sauce.

8. Lay on 2 slices of provolone, 2 slices of tomato, 2 slices of Cheddar . . .

9. A nice layer of roasted green chiles . . .

10. A few red onion slices . . .

11. And one more slice of provolone just to hold it all together. I'm structurally sound that way.

12. Top with the other slice of bread and spread the outsides with a good amount of butter. This is a fat-free sandwich. Not.

13. Toast the sandwich in a skillet over medium-low heat until the cheese is thoroughly melted inside. Be careful not to burn the bread!

14. Mmmmm. This is one beautiful sandwich. You'll absolutely love it.

Variation

Add a couple of slices of fried bacon to the sandwich. Yum!

Ol' Yeller is the oldest . . . and shortest . . . and yellowest horse on the ranch. My father-in-law loves him because he's easy to get on. My baby loves him for the same reason.

We have to travel on five miles of gravel road just to get to the highway. Tire companies have erected monuments in our honor.

CHIPOTLE STEAK SALAD

Makes 4 to 6 servings

I have a problem with steak salads: I love them. This isn't actually a problem at all, unless you call a complete inability to stop eating something until not a trace remains a problem. Which I do, and which I have. So as I said earlier: I have a problem.

This main-dish salad is divine. Angels will sing. It's a cinch to throw together, and the dressing is so spectacularly simple, you'll want to make extra so you can use it as a veggie dip or sandwich spread in the days and weeks to come. It's really tasty.

Let's make the salad! The angels are waiting in the wings . . . warming up their vocal cords.

Do you hear that? Do you hear the angels singing?

Sorry.

1 whole flank steak, 1½ to 2 pounds	One 7-ounce can chipotle peppers in adobo sauce	24 ounces salad greens (spring mix is best)
3 tablespoons olive oil	½ teaspoon ground cumin	4 roma tomatoes, sliced
1 tablespoon Worcestershire sauce	1 teaspoon dried oregano	1 cucumber, sliced
1 tablespoon honey	2 cups mayonnaise	1 red onion, halved and thinly sliced

1. Begin with a gorgeous flank steak or skirt steak, a cut of beef that usually needs to marinate for a while.

2. Add the olive oil to a bowl . . .

3. Then add the Worcestershire sauce, honey, and 2 tablespoons adobo sauce from the can of chipotle peppers. (And hang on to the rest of the can; we'll need them in a sec!)

7. While the meat is marinating, make the salad dressing, which is nothing but mayonnaise and the rest of the can of chipotle peppers!

11. To serve, mound the greens high on each plate and drape slices of warm meat down the sides.

4. Stir in the cumin and oregano . . .

8. Whirl the two together in a food processor or blender, then just stick it in the fridge till you need it.

12. Arrange tomato and cucumber slices around the sides of each plate, then top each salad with the red onion slices. Spoon the chipotle dressing all around the salad.

Cold lettuce + warm meat + cool dressing + crisp vegetables = bliss.

It's a mathematical certainty.

5. Then pour the marinade over the flank steak.

9. After the steak has marinated, grill it over a hot flame until medium rare, only about 2 minutes per side.

Variations

- *Use the chipotle dressing as a spicy veggie dip.*

- *Make a sandwich out of salad ingredients: spread chipotle dressing on the bread, then pile on the greens, the beef, and the cucumbers, onions, and tomatoes.*

6. Spread it on both sides of the meat, then cover and refrigerate the steak for a couple of hours at least.

10. Allow the meat to rest for 10 minutes, then slice it very thin (and on a slight diagonal) with a sharp knife.

BASIC CHICKEN SALAD

Makes 8 servings

Chicken salad is like a box of chocolates. You never know what you're gonna git.

This is chicken salad the way I like it! And my way is the best way. In my own mind. As far as I'm concerned. According to me.

½ cup mayonnaise

½ cup plain yogurt or sour cream

½ cup half-and-half

2 tablespoons lemon juice

2 tablespoons sugar

Kosher salt to taste

Freshly ground black pepper to taste

2 cups shredded or diced cooked chicken

2 or 3 celery stalks, chopped

3 green onions, sliced (white and light green parts only)

2 to 3 cups red and green grapes, halved

½ cup slivered almonds, lightly toasted in a small skillet until golden brown

A small handful of fresh dill, minced

Sandwich bread, croissants, store-bought crepes, lettuce, or radicchio, for serving

1. First, stir together the mayonnaise, yogurt, and half-and-half. This is the base of the chicken salad dressing, and you can change it up by adding whatever spices or ingredients you like.

2. Add the lemon juice . . .

3. Sugar . . .

4. And some salt and pepper.

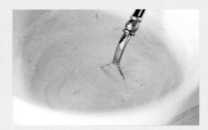

5. Stir this together and set it aside for a second. Okay, fine—37 seconds.

6. Throw the chicken, celery, green onions, and grapes into a bowl.

7. Pour three-quarters of the dressing over the top.

8. Toss it together, then toss in the slivered almonds . . .

9. And the fresh dill. Fresh dill makes chicken salad dreamy!

10. Give it a final toss and a final taste, adjusting whatever seasonings you think it needs and adding more dressing if it needs more moisture.

11. Wrap it inside a crepe or croissant, or between two slices of toasted bread, or serve it alone on a big leaf of lettuce or radicchio.

Cutie patootie!

CURRIED CHICKEN PASTA SALAD

Makes 8 to 10 servings

Use the Basic Chicken Salad recipe to create this gorgeous, colorful, and exceedingly flavorful curry pasta version, which you can serve by itself or wrapped in a crepe or flatbread. So, so wonderfully good.

1 recipe Basic Chicken Salad (page 50)

2 tablespoons brown sugar

3 tablespoons curry powder, more or less to taste

6 ounces bow tie pasta, cooked and drained

¾ cup regular or golden raisins

1. Mix up the Basic Chicken Salad dressing, substituting the brown sugar for the regular sugar. Stir in the curry powder.

2. In a large bowl, combine the chicken salad ingredients and the pasta, substituting the raisins for the grapes. Pour on the curry dressing . . .

3. And toss it around to combine.

Perfect chicken salad with a scrumptious curry kick! To die for.

A girl's gotta have choices.

SPICY GRILLED VEGETABLE PANINI

Makes 4 sandwiches

I love panini. I don't know what magical thing happens when you smash a loaded sandwich between two sides of a panini press, but I do know I like it.

This panini is so darn good, you'll seriously want to cry. When I make it, I always tell myself I'm only going to be able to eat half . . . and I wind up wolfing down the whole darn thing.

½ cup olive oil

¼ cup plus 2 tablespoons balsamic vinegar

Salt and black pepper to taste

1 yellow squash, cut into thick diagonal slices

1 zucchini, cut into thick diagonal slices

1 red bell pepper, seeded and cut into large chunks

1 yellow bell pepper, seeded and cut into large chunks

2 cups sliced button mushrooms

5 tablespoons butter

2 roma tomatoes, sliced

¼ cup mayonnaise

¼ cup hot pepper jelly (the spicier, the better!)

12 to 16 slices pepper jack cheese

8 thick slices crusty French bread

1. Make a marinade for the vegetables by combining the olive oil and ¼ cup of the balsamic vinegar in a large bowl.

3. Throw the squash, zucchini, and peppers into the bowl . . .

5. In a small skillet over medium-high heat, sauté the mushrooms in 1 tablespoon of the butter and the remaining 2 tablespoons balsamic vinegar until golden brown, about 5 minutes.

2. Add salt and pepper to taste and mix together.

4. And toss them together to coat. Set aside.

6. Remove the mushrooms to a plate and set aside.

7. Grill the vegetables on both sides until golden brown and tender.

9. For the panini spread, combine the mayonnaise and pepper jelly.

11. To assemble the sandwiches, spread each piece of bread with a generous amount of spread.

8. While the vegetables are grilling, toss the tomato slices in the marinade.

10. Stir it to combine.

12. Place 1 to 2 slices of cheese on each slice of bread.

My vegetable garden feeds my soul. And my belly. And a whole bunch of grasshoppers' bellies, unfortunately. Grrrrr.

13. To 4 slices of the bread, layer on some zucchini . . .

15. Some peppers and tomatoes . . .

17. Carefully bring the 2 halves of each sandwich together, spread the outsides with the remaining 4 tablespoons butter, and grill in a panini press until golden brown and the cheese is melted. (If you don't have a panini press, see page 57.)

Panini for president! This one definitely has my vote.

14. Some mushrooms . . .

16. And some squash.

Hint: Roast vegetables on a baking sheet in a 400°F oven until brown if you don't have access to a grill.

Variation

For a delicious alternative panini spread, mix 2 tablespoons Pesto (page 137) with 4 tablespoons mayonnaise.

CHICKEN APRICOT PANINI

Makes 4 sandwiches

This simple, but oh, so flavorful panini is one of my favorites.

2 boneless, skinless chicken breasts

3 tablespoons canola oil, for frying

6 tablespoons butter

Salt and black pepper to taste

12 to 16 fresh sage leaves

¼ cup apricot preserves

¼ cup mayonnaise

8 thick slices crusty French bread

½ red onion, thinly sliced

1. Begin by cutting the chicken breasts in half.

2. This is a quick and easy way to turn 1 chicken breast into 2 thinner pieces. Flatten them slightly if needed to fit the size of bread you're using.

3. In a large skillet over medium-high heat, heat the canola oil and 2 tablespoons of the butter. Add the chicken breasts to the skillet and cook until browned on one side, about 3 minutes.

4. Flip the chicken breasts and add some of the sage leaves to the hot oil. (Trust me! You won't believe what frying will do to the flavor.)

5. Flip them once, and when it looks like they're becoming crisp . . .

9. To build each sandwich, spoon a generous portion of the spread on a slice of bread.

13. Place a chicken breast on the onion . . .

6. Remove them from the skillet. Repeat with the rest of the sage leaves. Remove the chicken when it's cooked all the way through.

10. Spread it out . . .

14. Then flip the top piece of bread onto the chicken. Spread softened butter on both sides of the sandwich.

7. In a small bowl, add the apricot preserves and mayonnaise.

11. Then add some red onion to 1 slice . . .

15. Grill the sandwiches in a panini press, if you have one. If you don't, you can grill them in a skillet one at a time with a second (heavy) skillet on top of each sandwich to press it together. Just turn it halfway through to grill the other side as well.

8. Stir to combine. This is a scrumptious panini spread!

12. And sage leaves to the other.

This is one perfect panini!

SLOPPY JOES

Makes 8 servings

I used to be scared of Sloppy Joes when I was a little girl. I can't explain why. Hopefully I'll have answers someday. The good news is, I've since fallen in love with the drippy, meaty suckers. You'll fall in love with them, too! They've come a long way since the school cafeteria.

2½ pounds ground beef

1 large green bell pepper, diced

½ large onion, diced

5 garlic cloves, minced

1½ cups ketchup

2 tablespoons packed brown sugar

2 teaspoons chili powder, or more to taste

1 teaspoon dry mustard

½ teaspoon red pepper flakes, or more to taste

Worcestershire sauce to taste

Tabasco sauce to taste

Salt to taste

Freshly ground black pepper to taste

8 kaiser rolls

2 tablespoons butter

1. Start by browning the ground beef in a large pot over medium-high heat.

5. Ketchup . . .

9. Stir to combine, then cover and simmer over medium-low heat for 20 minutes.

2. Drain off the fat. Your cardiologist will give you a gold star.

6. And 1 cup water.

10. To serve, spread the kaiser rolls with softened butter and brown them on a griddle or skillet.

3. Then add in the green pepper and onion.

7. Stir it around to combine . . .

8. Then add the brown sugar, chili powder, mustard, red pepper flakes, Worcestershire sauce, Tabasco, salt, and pepper.

11. Spoon a good amount of the meat mixture onto the bottom roll, then top with the other half. Serve with chips, salad, or just enjoy it by itself.

See, Ree? There was nothing to be afraid of!

4. Stir, then add the minced garlic . . .

PERFECT SPINACH SALAD

Makes 6 servings

This glorious spinach salad is set apart from the typical spinach salad in two important ways: The red onions, which are usually sliced thin and added to spinach salad raw, are cooked until golden brown and tossed with the spinach. And the mushrooms, which are also usually sliced thin and added to the spinach salad raw, are . . . well . . . cooked until golden brown and tossed with the spinach. Crumbled bacon and sliced hard-boiled eggs make the whole thing worth living for.

We go way back, this spinach salad and me, and we've had a long, long time to get acquainted. I'd like to introduce you.

8 slices thick-cut bacon

4 tablespoons reserved bacon grease

1 red onion, thinly sliced

8 ounces cremini or white button mushrooms, sliced

4 hard-boiled eggs

3 tablespoons red wine vinegar

2 teaspoons sugar

½ teaspoon Dijon mustard

Dash of salt

12 ounces baby spinach, washed and dried

1. Fry the bacon until slightly crisp. Try with all your might not to eat it all before serving the salad. *Note: This will be difficult.* Drain the bacon on paper towels, then chop up the bacon and set it aside. Reserve the bacon grease.

2. Add 1 tablespoon of the bacon grease to a separate skillet over medium-low heat, then add the sliced onion . . .

3. And cook it slowly until it's nice and golden brown, about 10 minutes. Remove from the skillet and set aside.

4. Next, sauté the sliced mushrooms over medium-low heat in the same skillet until golden brown, about 10 minutes. Set aside.

5. Peel and slice the hard-boiled eggs. Take a whiff. Think of Easter.

6. Now make the dressing: Add 3 tablespoons of the remaining bacon grease, the red wine vinegar, sugar, Dijon, and salt.

7. Stir it with a fork to combine. Give it a taste and adjust the seasonings to make it all yours.

8. To assemble the salad, throw the beautiful spinach into a big ol' bowl.

9. Pile in the chopped bacon, caramelized red onion, sautéed mushrooms, and sliced eggs.

10. Drizzle on half of the yummy dressing, then toss the salad gently to mix all the ingredients together. Taste a spinach leaf and add more dressing as needed.

11. Arrange individual portions on plates and serve immediately.

Variations

• *Add 1 cup grated Swiss cheese to the salad.*

• *Add 1 cup diced cooked chicken or turkey.*

• *Add Cornbread Croutons (page 42).*

SIMPLE SESAME NOODLES

Makes 8 to 10 servings

Sometimes simple is best, and these sesame noodles fall under that umbrella. You can pair them with delicious roasted beef tenderloin. You can load them with red bell pepper, fresh cilantro, or chopped cooked shrimp.

Or you can eat them unadorned. They're utterly perfect just the way they are.

12 ounces thin noodles, such as angel hair, spaghetti, or lo mein

¼ cup soy sauce

2 tablespoons sugar

4 garlic cloves, minced

2 tablespoons rice vinegar

3 tablespoons toasted sesame oil

½ teaspoon hot chili oil

4 tablespoons canola oil

4 green onions, thinly sliced (white and light green parts only)

1. Cook the noodles according to package directions. Drain and set aside.

4. Rice vinegar . . .

2. While the noodles are cooking, mix together the soy sauce, sugar . . .

5. Sesame oil, hot chili oil . . .

3. Garlic . . .

6. Canola oil, and ¼ cup water.

7. Stir it together and pour it over the warm noodles.

8. Toss to coat all the noodles, then toss in the sliced green onions.

9. You can eat this immediately or you can refrigerate the noodles for several hours and enjoy them as a cool salad.

Variation
SESAME BEEF NOODLE SALAD

Makes 8 servings

Use a little of the dressing from Simple Sesame Noodles to marinate a grilled steak and turn it into this delicious cold salad.

One ½-inch-thick sirloin steak

Dressing from Simple Sesame Noodles (page 62)

8 ounces thin noodles (such as angel hair, spaghetti, or lo mein), cooked and drained

1 cup cilantro leaves

4 green onions, thinly sliced (white and light green parts only)

2. Place the steak inside a plastic bag and add 2 to 3 tablespoons of the dressing. Stick it in the fridge and allow it to marinate for at least a couple of hours.

4. Toss the cooked noodles with the rest of the dressing, then toss in the cilantro leaves.

1. Grill the steak until medium rare, about 2 minutes per side (or use any leftover steak you might have).

3. Slice the steak against the grain.

5. Dish the noodles into bowls, then lay strips of beef on top and sprinkle with the green onions. A perfectly delicious lunch!

DRIP BEEF

Makes 10 to 12 servings

I learned to make this drip beef from my best friend Hyacinth. It's a delicious, slow-cooked concoction designed to be slapped onto a deli roll. The juices "drip" onto the bottom half of the bun, and the flavor is seriously beyond measure.

One 3- to 4-pound chuck roast
Salt and black pepper to taste
2 tablespoons butter
2 tablespoons canola oil

2 cups beef broth
2 tablespoons minced fresh rosemary
1 jar peperoncinis

10 to 12 buttered, toasted deli rolls
2 yellow onions, sliced and sautéed in 1 tablespoon butter until light golden brown

1. Season the chuck roast with salt and pepper.

2. Melt the butter and canola oil in a heavy pot over high heat. Sear both sides of the chuck roast until very browned, about 5 minutes in all.

3. Pour in the beef broth and 1 cup water.

7. Using 2 forks, shred the meat completely . . .

11. And plenty of caramelized onions.

4. Add the rosemary . . .

8. Then return the meat to the cooking liquid. Keep warm.

5. Then pour in the peperoncinis with their juice. Now cover the pot and simmer for 4 to 5 hours, or until the meat is tender and falling apart.

9. To serve, slice wedges out of the top of the deli rolls. Heap a generous portion of meat on the roll, then spoon some of the cooking liquid over the meat.

12. Top the sandwiches with the wedges of roll and serve to a roomful of ravenous guests. You'll win friends and influence people.

Like, totally.

Variations

- *Lay thinly sliced cheese on top of the meat before adding the peppers and onions.*
- *Serve dishes of the cooking liquid on the side for dipping.*

6. Remove the roast from the pot.

10. Top with a few peppers from the pot . . .

BEEF AND BEAN BURRITOS

6 to 8 servings

This is one of those recipes you whip out when your kids (or your husband . . . or your wife . . . or your mailman) are banging their forks on the table looking for something brown, hot, and satisfying to eat. The little bean-and-beef numbers take exactly sixteen minutes to get on the table (give or take an hour. Just kidding), and considering how simple they are to make, it's almost hilarious how popular they are in my house.

2 pounds ground beef

1 medium onion, diced

½ teaspoon ground cumin

¼ teaspoon ground oregano

¼ teaspoon chili powder

¼ teaspoon salt

Two 7-ounce cans Mexican tomato sauce (I use El Pato brand) or enchilada sauce

One 28-ounce can refried beans

¾ cup grated Cheddar cheese, plus extra for sprinkling

12 burrito-size flour tortillas

OPTIONAL FILLING INGREDIENTS

Mexican Rice (page 173), sour cream, guacamole, roasted green chiles, pico de gallo

½ cup cilantro leaves

1. In a large skillet over medium heat, cook the ground beef and onion until the beef is cooked through. Add the cumin, oregano, chili powder, and salt and stir to combine.

Here's the sauce I use. It's sold in the Hispanic foods section of the grocery store. I love it. Amen.

2. Pour 1 can of the sauce into the meat and simmer over low heat for 5 minutes. Add a little water if the mixture gets too dry.

3. Meanwhile, heat the refried beans in a saucepan over medium-low heat.

4. Add the cheese . . .

5. And stir it in till it's melted. Remove from the heat.

6. Heat the tortillas in the microwave for 1 minute, then spread a small amount of beans on each tortilla.

7. Add a small amount of the meat. Add any other optional ingredients you may be using, or just leave 'em as they are!

8. Fold over the ends of the tortilla . . .

9. Then roll them up. Place 2 burritos on a microwave-safe plate.

10. Drizzle some of the second can of red sauce over the top . . .

11. And sprinkle with more grated Cheddar.

12. Microwave the burritos for 1 minute, or until the cheese is melted. Repeat with the rest of the burritos.

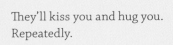

13. Sprinkle the tops with cilantro leaves and serve immediately to the fork-bangers in your life.

They'll kiss you and hug you. Repeatedly.

SOUPS

GAZPACHO

Makes 8 servings

I've had a love affair with gazpacho since I saw the movie *Violets Are Blue* with Kevin Kline and Sissy Spacek. As Bonnie Bedelia explains right before serving it to Sissy Spacek, just hours before Sissy is about to commit an indiscretion with her husband, Kevin, gazpacho is "salad in a blender." It's *not* a cooked tomato soup that's served cold. It's a raw cold soup: fresh, textured, light, and such a delicious summer treat. I love it more every time I eat it. It just feels good.

Not that "it just feels good" is a reason to do anything! You hear that, Sissy and Kevin? Tsk, tsk, tsk.

1 pound shrimp, peeled and deveined

2 garlic cloves, minced

½ red onion

1 large cucumber

1 zucchini

2 celery stalks

5 roma tomatoes

¼ cup extra-virgin olive oil

2 tablespoons red wine vinegar

2 tablespoons sugar

Several dashes of hot sauce

Dash of salt

Dash of black pepper

4 cups good-quality tomato juice

Avocado slices

2 hard-boiled eggs, finely minced

Cilantro leaves

Crusty bread, for serving

1. Begin by grilling or sautéing the shrimp until opaque. Set aside.

2. Mince up the garlic.

3. Cut the onion into slices.

4. Dice up the cucumber . . .

5. The zucchini . . .

6. The celery . . .

7. And the tomatoes. Everything's so fresh and colorful!

8. Throw all the garlic, all the onion, half the vegetables, and the olive oil into the bowl of a food processor or, if you want to be like Bonnie Bedelia, a blender.

9. Splash in the red wine vinegar, and add the sugar . . .

10. The hot sauce . . .

11. And salt and pepper.

12. Finally, pour in 2 cups of the tomato juice and blend well. You'll basically have a tomato base with a beautiful confetti of vegetables.

13. Pour the blended mixture into a large bowl and add in the other half of the vegetables.

15. Then stir in the remaining 2 cups tomato juice. Give it a taste and make sure the seasoning is right. Adjust it as needed.

14. Stir it together . . .

Country ponds are perfect for budding scientists. Even those without shirts.

16. Ladle the soup into bowls and top with the grilled shrimp. Garnish with avocado slices, hard-boiled egg, and cilantro leaves. Serve with crusty bread on the side.

You've gotta try it, my friends. It's one of the most perfect summer treats there is.

CORN CHOWDER

Makes 10 to 12 servings

I love fresh corn shaved right off the cob, and this thick, creamy chowder is loaded with the stuff. For a nice flavor twist, I add chipotle peppers and chopped green chiles . . . and I thicken the soup at the end with a little cornmeal. This creamy, hearty soup is absolutely *ta-die-fer*.

5 ears of corn, shucked

2 slices bacon, cut into ½-inch pieces (or smaller)

1 medium yellow onion, diced

2 to 3 whole chipotle peppers in adobo sauce, finely diced

4 cups (1 quart) low-sodium chicken broth

1½ cups heavy whipping cream

One 4-ounce can diced green chiles

3 tablespoons cornmeal

Salt to taste

Warm corn tortillas, for serving

1. Corn chowder starts . . . with corn! Aren't you glad you have me here to tell you these things?

2. With a sharp knife, slice off the kernels from the cob.

3. Next, cut some bacon into 1-inch pieces. I like to just open up a package and lop an inch off the whole thing. Easier that way.

4. Cook the bacon pieces in a large pot over medium heat until the fat begins to render, about 2 minutes.

5. Add the diced onion to the pot and cook it until the onion is translucent and the bacon is cooked but still chewy, about 5 minutes.

6. Next, throw in the corn kernels. Stir them around and allow them to begin cooking.

7. Crack open a can of chipotle peppers. Chipotles are my life these days. I'll pretty much add them to anything! Except perhaps my bowl of Cocoa Puffs.

8. Mince up a couple of peppers . . .

9. Then stir them into the corn. Continue cooking for about 3 minutes.

10. After that, pour in the low-sodium chicken broth . . .

11. Followed by a nice, healthy (healthy?) splash of heavy cream. And okay, it's more than a splash.

12. Stir this around to combine.

13. Add the green chiles. Adds a wonderful flavor!

15. At that point, mix the cornmeal with ¼ cup water and stir together.

14. Let the soup simmer for 25 to 30 minutes.

16. Stir the mixture into the soup and simmer for another 10 minutes, or until thickened. Taste and add salt if needed.

17. Serve in bowls with warm corn tortillas on the side.

So warm. So creamy. So corny. In a very, very, very good way.

Heeeeeeeeeeeeeere's WALTER!

CHICKEN TORTILLA SOUP

Makes 8 servings

This delicious, hearty, slightly spicy Tex-Mex soup will knock your socks off. Garnish it with avocado, sour cream . . . and pretty much anything else that you can come up with! The flavors in this soup are out of this world.

1½ teaspoons ground cumin

About 1¼ teaspoons chili powder

½ teaspoon garlic powder

½ teaspoon salt, plus more to taste

2 boneless, skinless chicken breasts

2 tablespoons olive oil

1 cup diced onion

3 garlic cloves, minced

¼ cup diced green bell pepper

¼ cup diced red bell pepper

One 10-ounce can Rotel Diced Tomatoes and Green Chiles

4 cups (1 quart) low-sodium chicken broth

3 tablespoons tomato paste

4 cups hot water

Two 15-ounce cans black beans, drained

3 tablespoons cornmeal

5 small corn tortillas

Diced avocado, for garnish

Diced red onion, for garnish

Sour cream, for garnish

Chopped cilantro, for garnish

1. Preheat the oven to 375°F.

2. Start by mixing together the cumin, 1 teaspoon of the chili powder, the garlic powder, and salt.

3. Drizzle the chicken breasts with 1 tablespoon of the olive oil. (Here, I'm cooking some extra breasts to keep in the fridge and use throughout the week.)

4. Then sprinkle with 1 teaspoon of the spice mixture. Set the rest of the spice mixture aside.

5. Bake for 15 to 20 minutes, or until the chicken is cooked all the way through. Remove it from the oven . . .

6. And shred the chicken using 2 forks. Set aside.

7. Next, heat the remaining 1 tablespoon of olive oil in a large pot over medium-high heat. Throw in the onion, garlic, and green and red bell peppers.

8. Throw in a teaspoon of the spice mixture used to season the chicken.

9. Add a little extra chili powder (about ¼ teaspoon) for heat.

10. Stir to cook the vegetables until they begin to turn golden brown, about 5 minutes.

11. Add the shredded chicken . . .

12. The Rotel, juice and all.

13. The chicken broth . . .

14. The tomato paste, and 4 cups hot water. Stir to combine and bring the mixture to a boil. Reduce the heat to low.

15. Next, add the drained black beans.

16. Then mix together the cornmeal with ½ cup of water.

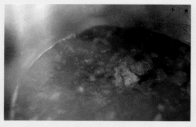

17. Add the mixture to the pot, then simmer the soup for 10 to 15 minutes. Give it a taste and add salt or seasonings as needed; be sure not to undersalt it!

18. Cut the tortillas into uniform 2- to 3-inch strips.

19. Stir them into the soup. This is what makes tortilla soup *tortilla soup*! Turn off the heat and get ready to serve it up.

20. Ladle the soup into a bowl, then add avocado, red onion, sour cream, cilantro, and extra tortilla strips to the top. The more toppings on tortilla soup, the merrier.

OTHER SUGGESTED TOPPINGS

- Grated Monterey Jack cheese
- Pico de gallo
- Grilled Corn Guacamole (page 90)

Variation

Omit the chicken and use vegetable broth for a veggie-only soup.

"I am in love with this world." —John Burroughs

ITALIAN MEATBALL SOUP

Makes 10 to 12 servings

This gorgeous soup, loaded with tangy tomato, crunchy cabbage, and magnificent meatballs, comes from my beautiful mother. Wait. I mean this *wonderful* soup comes from my *delicious* mother. Wait. I mean this *delicious* soup comes from my *wonderful* mother. Wait . . .

Oh, never mind.

Here's the beautiful, gorgeous, delicious, wonderful recipe. (Thanks, Mom!)

¾ **pound ground beef**

1 large egg

2 garlic cloves

7 tablespoons minced fresh parsley

2 teaspoons lemon juice

¼ **teaspoon salt, plus more to taste**

½ **teaspoon black pepper**

¼ **teaspoon ground oregano**

½ **cup freshly grated Parmesan cheese, plus more for serving**

3 tablespoons olive oil

7 cups low-sodium beef stock

2 heaping tablespoons tomato paste

2 whole bay leaves

1 teaspoon peppercorns

¾ **cup diced onion**

¾ **cup diced carrots**

¾ **cup diced celery**

1 cup diced russet potato

½ **pound cabbage, sliced**

Crusty bread, for serving

1. To make the meatballs, add the ground beef, egg, garlic, 3 tablespoons of the parsley, the lemon juice, salt, pepper, ground oregano, and grated Parmesan to a bowl.

2. Mix together well . . .

3. Then roll the mixture into 1-inch balls.

4. In a large pot, heat the olive oil over medium-high heat. Brown the meatballs in batches, turning to brown, 3 to 4 minutes per batch. No need to cook them all the way, as they'll go back into the soup later.

5. When the meatballs are brown, remove them with a slotted spoon and set aside.

6. Now, grab some beef stock . . .

7. And pour it into the pot.

8. Add some salt. (Don't be confused by how dark the soup looks in this photo. It's an exposure thing. The world, and my photography, is an imperfect beast.)

9. Stir in the tomato paste. Adds so much yummy richness.

10. Next, make a bouquet garni, which is pronounced "bow-kay gar-nee" 'round these parts. Add the remaining 4 tablespoons parsley, the bay leaves, and peppercorns to a piece of cheesecloth and tie it into a bundle using kitchen twine.

11. Drop it right into the soup. Adds incredible flavor!

12. Bring the soup to a boil, then reduce the heat and let it simmer for 30 minutes.

13. Remove the bouquet garni, which now resembles a jellyfish with jaundice, from the pot. Go ahead and discard it. It's lived a full life.

14. Next, add the diced vegetables . . .

15. And the crisp, sliced cabbage.

16. Finally, in go the browned meatballs.

17. Let the soup simmer for another 20 minutes or so, long enough for the vegetables to get slightly tender and the meatballs to cook all the way through.

18. You can sprinkle the soup with some freshly grated Parmesan if you'd like one last dose of decadence. A loaf of crusty bread is a must!

You'll absolutely love this soup.

You'd love my mother, too, if you ever met her. She's pretty groovy, man.

(Hi, Mom!)

"I am in love with this man." —Pioneer Woman

CHICKEN AND NOODLES

Makes 8 to 10 servings

Chicken and Noodles is a plunge into my childhood. My mom and grandmother used to make it regularly, and it's been a lifelong favorite of mine.

Though a batch of homemade noodles was occasionally a part of the picture, both homegirls usually settled on frozen store-bought noodles, which are typically made from only flour, water, and eggs. It's a shortcut that makes this dish a total cinch while keeping it wholesome and heavenly . . . emphasis on divine.

One 2- to 3-pound chicken fryer, cut up

½ medium onion, diced

2 celery stalks, diced

2 carrots, diced

1 teaspoon salt

¼ teaspoon white pepper

½ teaspoon turmeric

¼ teaspoon ground thyme

2 teaspoons finely minced parsley

16 ounces frozen homestyle egg noodles

3 tablespoons all-purpose flour

Splash of half-and-half (optional)

1. Start by putting the chicken in a pot and covering it with water. Bring the water to a boil, then reduce the heat to low. Simmer for 45 minutes, then remove the chicken from the pot. Set the chicken aside to cool briefly.

2. Shred the chicken with 2 forks, reserving the bones.

3. Return the bones to the pot and boil for 20 minutes. Remove the bones from the pot and discard.

4. Add the shredded chicken, onion, celery, and carrots to the pot.

5. Then add the salt, pepper, turmeric, thyme, and minced parsley.

6. Bring the mixture to a gentle boil, then reduce the heat and simmer for 10 minutes.

7. Stir in the noodles. No need to thaw them first!

8. Finally, mix the flour with ½ cup water until smooth. Stir the flour mixture and the splash of half-and-half (if you're into that kind of thing) into the pot. Simmer for 15 minutes, or until the noodles are tender, tasting and adding more salt if needed at the end.

9. The soup should be thick and stewlike . . .

And your kitchen should smell like home.

FRENCH ONION SOUP

Makes 8 servings

There are few things that make me want to live year-round in a freezing cold climate more than French Onion Soup. The oniony-beefy broth . . . the crouton . . . the crown of melted cheese. Whoever invented this soup is my hero.

4 large yellow onions

½ cup (1 stick) butter

1 cup (generous) dry white wine

4 cups (1 quart) low-sodium chicken broth

4 cups (1 quart) low-sodium beef broth

4 to 5 dashes of Worcestershire sauce

2 garlic cloves, minced

Several thick slices French bread or baguette, drizzled with olive oil and toasted

8 ounces Gruyère or Swiss cheese, sliced thick

1. Preheat the oven to 400°F.

2. Slice the onions in half from root to tip, then slice them up.

3. Melt the butter in a heavy pot or Dutch oven over medium-low heat.

4. Add the onions, stir to coat them with butter, then cook them, covered, for 20 minutes, or until they are translucent and soft. Place the pot into the oven with the lid slightly ajar.

5. Roast the onions for 1 hour, stirring twice to keep them from burning. (Some dark parts, as shown above, are fine.)

6. Return the pot to the stovetop over medium heat and pour in the wine. Stir, scraping the pan. Cook for 5 minutes, or until the wine reduces.

7. Next, add the chicken broth . . .

8. The beef broth . . .

9. The Worcestershire sauce . . .

10. And the garlic.

11. Reduce the heat to low and let the soup simmer for 45 minutes.

12. To serve, turn on the broiler. Ladle the soup into ovenproof bowls. Place 1 or 2 pieces of the toasted bread on top of the soup, depending on the size of the bowl.

13. I put in a little extra. I like carbs.

14. Place a thick slice of cheese on top of each bowl, then place the bowls on a cookie sheet and broil just long enough for the cheese to become melted, bubbly, and slightly toasted on top.

Close your eyes. Savor the moment. Grab your spoon. Dig in!

Variation

For a deeper flavor and color, substitute red wine for the white wine.

CAULIFLOWER SOUP

Makes 10 to 12 servings

Out of all the soups in my soupertoire, the one that most says *comfort food* to me is my soupmaster mom's time-tested Cauliflower Soup. It's brothy. Savory. Creamy. Filled with tender chunks of cauliflower and all the goodness of life. I've made it in my own household for years, and I love it as much now as I did when I was a young girl with frizzy hair, sun-bleached eyebrows, and a wicked crush on Robbie Benson.

Keep in mind that while this soup may appear to have a lot of steps, there's nothing difficult about it. Just get your ingredients ready ahead of time and it'll be a cinch.

1 stick butter

½ onion, finely diced

1 carrot, finely diced

1 celery stalk, finely diced

1 cauliflower head, cored and roughly chopped

2 tablespoons finely minced fresh parsley

2 quarts low-sodium chicken broth or stock

6 tablespoons all-purpose flour

2 cups whole milk

1 cup half-and-half

1 to 2 teaspoons salt, or to taste

Black pepper to taste

1 heaping cup sour cream, at room temperature

Crusty bread, for serving

2. Add the carrot and celery . . .

4. Throw in the cauliflower . . .

3. Then stir and cook for a couple more minutes.

5. Then stir it around, cover, and cook over very low heat for 15 minutes.

1. Melt ½ stick butter in a heavy pot over medium heat, then add the onion and cook until translucent, about 3 minutes.

6. Use your very strange-looking, freaky pink alien claw to add the finely minced parsley.

What's up with my hand in this photo? I need to know more.

I also need a hand model.

7. Then add the chicken broth and simmer for 10 minutes. I'd like to publicly thank my hand for staying out of this photo.

8. Meantime, make a simple white sauce: Melt the remaining ½ stick of butter in a medium saucepan over medium heat, then whisk in the flour. Cook for a couple of minutes, then pour in the milk, whisking to combine.

9. Remove the white sauce from the heat and pour in the half-and-half.

10. Then pour this creamy mixture into the pot.

11. Add 1 teaspoon salt and pepper to taste, and allow the soup to simmer for another 20 to 30 minutes. The soup will thicken slightly but shouldn't be overly thick. Give it a taste and add more salt if needed.

12. Now, this is the fun part: To serve the soup, place the room temperature sour cream in the bottom of a soup tureen (or a very large serving bowl).

13. Then add the whole pot of hot soup to the tureen.

14. Stir gently to combine, then serve immediately with warm rolls and an appetite for something wonderful.

You will love everything about this.

Variation

For a smoother, thicker soup, use an immersion blender to puree. Simmer an additional 10 minutes after pureeing.

Boing!

STARTERS, PARTY FOOD, AND DRINKS

GRILLED CORN GUACAMOLE

Makes 8 servings

Adding grilled corn to a basic guacamole gives it an amazing texture and lovely sweetness that makes it even more irresistible than regular guacamole. A touch of cumin catapults it into the heavens. A margarita and a Jimmy Buffett song would make life too perfect to handle.

3 ears of sweet corn

6 avocados

⅓ cup finely diced onion

2 garlic cloves, finely minced

1 large tomato, diced

2 tablespoons diced fresh jalapeño

½ teaspoon kosher salt

¼ teaspoon ground cumin

Juice of 1 lime

½ cup cilantro leaves

Tortilla chips, for serving

1. Begin by grilling the ears of corn until the kernels start to turn golden brown.

2. Let the corn cool slightly, then use a very sharp knife to shave the kernels off the cob.

3. Slice the avocados in half and remove the pits.

4. Use a knife to cut each half into a dice . . .

5. Then use a spoon to scoop the pieces into a bowl.

6. Now add the corn . . .

7. The onion, garlic, tomato, and jalapeño . . .

8. And the salt, cumin, and lime juice.

9. Stir everything together until it's all combined and harmonious . . .

10. Then stir in the cilantro at the end. Taste the guacamole to make sure the seasonings are right.

11. Serve this treat with tortilla chips. Smiles will suddenly appear.

(Smiles are one of the direct effects of guacamole.)

Variations

Serve with Quesadillas de Camarones (page 156) or Barbecue Chicken and Pineapple Quesadillas (page 154), or atop Chicken Tortilla Soup (page 76), His/Her Burgers (page 160), or Mushroom Swiss Sliders (page 100).

RESTAURANT-STYLE SALSA

Makes 12 servings

Fact: I am extremely high maintenance when it comes to salsa.

As ubiquitous as it is, you'd think salsa would be a pretty straightforward thing. But it isn't. It's tricky. Crafty. Mischievous. When it comes to a good salsa, here's my list of demands:

No big chunks, man! Big chunks are good when it comes to the fresh tomatoes in pico de gallo. But when it comes to regular salsa, which is generally made from canned tomatoes, I prefer more of a pureed, thin consistency.

No vinegar, dude! At all. Vinegar does not belong in salsa, which is why I'm not a big fan of salsa from a jar. Most of it contains vinegar as a preservative. Grody!

Must have cilantro, pal! Lots and lots of cilantro.

But other than that, I'm totally adaptable when it comes to salsa.

One 28-ounce can whole tomatoes with juice

Two 10-ounce cans Rotel Diced Tomatoes and Green Chilies

¼ cup chopped onion

1 jalapeño

1 garlic clove, minced

¼ teaspoon sugar

¼ teaspoon salt

¼ teaspoon ground cumin

Juice of half a lime

½ cup cilantro (more to taste!)

1. Into a food processor or blender, add the whole tomatoes with their juice . . .

2. The Rotel . . .

3. And the onion.

4. Quarter the jalapeño lengthwise, then slice it thinly.

5. Add the jalapeño and garlic to the mix.

6. Next, add the sugar, salt, cumin . . .

7. Lime juice . . .

8. And cilantro.

9. Pulse several times until it reaches the consistency you like. You can just let 'er rip and puree the heck out of it, or you can leave it a little more chunky. The choice is yours!

Serve with chips!
Warning: May be habit forming.

Variations

Serve with Breakfast Pizza (page 26), White Chicken Enchiladas (page 186), Barbecue Chicken and Pineapple Quesadillas (page 154), Quesadillas de Camarones (page 156), or Tequila Lime Chicken (page 170).

HUMMUS

Makes 8 servings

I love hummus so much, I want to marry it. I think we'd be very happy together.

You can buy premade hummus in the grocery store, but it's never ever as good as it is when you make it yourself. An essential ingredient is tahini, a sesame paste. Most supermarkets have it these days!

Three 14.5-ounce cans chickpeas (garbanzo beans)

3 garlic cloves, peeled

Juice of 2 lemons

½ cup tahini

½ teaspoon ground cumin, or more to taste

¼ teaspoon cayenne pepper, or more to taste

½ teaspoon salt, or more to taste

¼ teaspoon black pepper

½ cup to 1 cup cold water

2 tablespoons olive oil

Freshly chopped flat-leaf parsley, for garnish

Carrot sticks, cucumber slices, kalamata olives, crackers, and/or breadsticks, for serving

1. Drain and rinse the chickpeas and throw them into the blender.

2. Add the garlic, lemon juice . . .

3. Tahini . . .

4. Cumin . . .

5. Cayenne . . .

6. Salt . . .

7. And pepper.

8. Blend the mixture, pouring in cold water as you go, starting with ½ cup and adding more as needed to get the consistency you want.

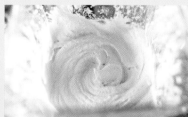

9. You may have to stop and give it a stir if the mixture becomes too thick. Just keep adding a little water here and there until it's right.

10. At the end, add the olive oil and give it a final pulse. Taste the hummus to make sure the seasoning is right.

11. Place the hummus in a dish, garnish it with parsley, and serve with carrots, cucumbers, olives, and crackers and/or breadsticks.

Hummus keeps well in the fridge, so you can make it a couple of days before you need it!

Variations

- *Add 3 to 4 roasted red peppers before blending for red pepper hummus.*

- *Use hummus as a spread on turkey or veggie sandwiches.*

BRIE-STUFFED MUSHROOMS

Makes about 16 to 18 mushrooms

You'll love these elegant (but very simple) stuffed mushrooms. They're beautiful and decadent and divine, and are the perfect little bite to serve before a dinner party. Guests will kiss you and demand to be invited back next time.

   (Whether or not you invite them back is entirely up to you and outside the scope of my involvement. I just wanted to mention it.)

12 ounces white button mushrooms, washed

½ stick butter

¼ cup chopped flat-leaf parsley

4 garlic cloves, minced

4 or 5 green onions, sliced (up to the middle of the dark green part)

Splash of white wine (optional)

One 8-ounce wedge Brie cheese, cut into bite-size chunks

1. Preheat the oven to 350°F.

2. Remove the stems from the mushrooms.

3. Melt the butter in a large skillet over medium-high heat.

4. When the butter is melted and the skillet is hot, throw in the mushroom caps and toss them around for a minute.

5. Remove the mushrooms from the skillet and set them aside. Throw in the parsley, garlic, and green onions. Add the wine if you're using it. Stir and cook for 1 to 2 minutes to release all the flavors, then remove from the heat.

6. Place the mushroom caps in a baking dish.

7. Place a chunk of Brie inside of each cap . . .

8. Then pour the parsley mixture all over the top.

9. Bake the mushrooms for 15 minutes, or until the cheese is melted. Serve them straight out of the oven or at room temperature a little bit later.

These are perfect little pop-in-your-mouth delights. You'll love them.

Variations

- *Use a combination of herbs (parsley, basil, sage) on the mushrooms.*

- *Use chunks of fresh mozzarella instead of Brie.*

- *Place a few stuffed mushrooms in between 2 slices of crusty French bread: stuffed mushroom sandwich!*

CAPRESE SALAD

Makes 8 to 12 servings

If something better than Caprese Salad exists on Earth, I haven't yet found what it is. In fact, I challenge anyone to show me something better than Caprese Salad! Go ahead. I'll wait.

See? You couldn't do it. I tried to tell you to save you the effort!

I love Caprese Salad. I love it in the morning and I love it in the night. I love it as a main-dish salad for lunch, and I love it as a side dish for dinner. I love it as a midnight snack, and I love it as a midafternoon snack, and I love it as a mid-late-early-dinner snack.

Have I mentioned I love Caprese Salad? Oh, good. I thought I'd forgotten.

This is a good one. The thick, glossy balsamic reduction makes for a gorgeous presentation and rich flavor. Try it sometime soon!

2 cups balsamic vinegar

3 ripe tomatoes

12 ounces fresh mozzarella cheese, thickly sliced

Fresh basil leaves

Olive oil, for drizzling

Kosher salt and freshly ground black pepper

1. Measure the balsamic vinegar . . .

2. And pour it into a saucepan.

3. Bring it to a gentle boil over low heat.

4. Cook it for about 15 minutes, or until the balsamic has reduced to a nice, thick (but still pourable) glaze. Oh, and one other thing: Your house will stink. But it's a good kind of stink. It's a vinegar kind of stink.

I'll stop talking now. Just allow the reduction to cool to room temperature before you serve it.

5. When you're ready to assemble the salad, cut the tomatoes into thick slices.

6. Arrange them on a platter, alternating them with the mozzarella slices.

7. Tuck whole basil leaves in between the tomato and cheese slices.

8. Drizzle olive oil in a thin stream over the top.

9. Then drizzle on the gorgeous, almost-black balsamic reduction.

10. Finally, sprinkle salt and pepper on top.

You need this in your life. Make it today, my friends.

Variations

- Use different varieties of heirloom tomatoes for a beautiful presentation.

- Substitute peach slices for the tomatoes for a sweeter salad.

- Use leftovers to make a Caprese sandwich. Spread Pesto (page 137) on the bread and add chopped Greek olives to send it over the top.

When I first saw my husband on a horse, I remember thinking there was no more beautiful sight in the world. Then I saw my baby on a horse, and it was all over.

MUSHROOM SWISS SLIDERS WITH SPICY FRY SAUCE

Makes 12 sliders

I love these flavorful, miraculous little hamburgers topped with winey mushrooms and melted Swiss. As if the aforementioned goodness wouldn't be more than enough, I also slather a spicy fry sauce on the buns. For those of you who don't know what fry sauce is . . . then you've never been to Utah or eaten French fries late at night in a college dorm mess hall. (Fry sauce is nothing more than ketchup mixed with mayonnaise. Perfect for a wicked case of the munchies.)

⅓ cup mayonnaise

2 tablespoons ketchup

1 teaspoon cayenne pepper (less if you're sensitive to spice!)

8 ounces white button mushrooms, finely chopped

½ medium onion, finely diced

4 tablespoons butter

½ cup white or red wine (optional)

8 dashes of Worcestershire sauce

Kosher salt and freshly ground black pepper

2½ pounds ground beef

¼ cup heavy whipping cream

6 slices Swiss cheese, cut into 4 squares each

12 dinner (or slider) rolls, split and toasted

1. Let's start with the good stuff: Add the mayonnaise and ketchup to a small bowl.

2. Add cayenne pepper (or hot sauce; whatever you prefer) . . .

3. And stir it until it's all combined. Set aside.

4. Next, chop up the mushrooms . . .

5. And half an onion.

6. Melt 3 tablespoons of the butter in a skillet over medium-high heat. Add the onion and sauté for a minute . . .

7. Then add the mushrooms. Stir them around and cook them for a minute.

8. Then pour in the wine (or use chicken or beef stock if you prefer). Add half the Worcestershire and salt and pepper to taste.

9. Cook until the mushrooms are soft and the wine has evaporated and reduced. Set aside.

10. Add the ground beef to a separate bowl. Then pour in the heavy cream. I won't tell anyone!

11. Add 1 teaspoon kosher salt, pepper to taste, and the remaining Worcestershire sauce, then stir or knead to combine it all.

12. Divide the beef into 12 portions and form them into patties.

13. Make a small indentation in the top of each patty. This'll keep the sliders from poufing up too much when they cook.

17. Use a scoop to add a big mound of the mushroom/onion mixture to each patty . . .

14. Sizzle the remaining tablespoon of butter in the skillet over medium heat.

18. Then lay 2 squares of Swiss cheese on top of each patty. Leave in the pan until the cheese melts.

20. Sandwich the patty in between the buns. Serve with onion rings or fries, along with some extra fry sauce for dipping!

Splendidly yummy.

Variations

Create a toppings bar for the sliders using avocado slices, crumbled bacon, pico de gallo, Restaurant-Style Salsa (page 92), blue cheese crumbles, and so on. Perfect for game day!

15. Cook sliders 4 to 6 at a time . . .

19. To serve, generously spread the top and bottom buns with fry sauce.

How now . . . white cow?

16. Until just about done, 3 to 4 minutes per side.

MEATBALL SLIDERS

Use leftover meatballs and sauce to make fun little meatball sliders. Serve with a green salad and a cold bottle of beer.

Unless they're for your kids. Then root beer will do just fine.

Leftover meatballs (see page 112 or 126) and sauce

Small slider buns or dinner rolls, split

Mozzarella cheese slices

Reheat the meatballs and sauce thoroughly, then spoon onto the bottom of the buns. Lay on a slice of mozzarella, then top with the other half of the bun.

FRIED MOZZARELLA

Makes 32 pieces

Homemade fried mozzarella couldn't be easier to make . . . or more delicious! Panko bread crumbs make them crispy, light, and wonderful.

Please be careful when frying with hot oil.

16 pieces string cheese, removed from their wrappers

½ cup all-purpose flour

2 eggs

¼ cup milk

2 cups panko bread crumbs

1 tablespoon dried parsley flakes

Canola oil, for frying

Marinara sauce, for dipping

1. Slice the string cheese pieces in half, for a total of 32 pieces.

2. Place the flour in a small bowl.

3. In a separate bowl, whisk together the eggs and milk.

4. In another bowl, combine the bread crumbs with the parsley flakes.

5. One by one, roll the mozzarella pieces in the flour . . .

6. Then briefly dunk them in the egg/milk mixture . . .

7. Finally, roll them in the panko mixture. Use your hands if necessary to get the crumbs to adhere.

8. Place the mozzarella pieces on a baking sheet, then place them in the freezer for 20 to 30 minutes to flash freeze.

9. To fry the mozzarella, heat 1½ inches of canola oil in a large skillet over medium-high heat. When the oil is hot, add the mozzarella sticks 6 to 8 pieces at a time. Watch them closely and turn them over to brown evenly. They should cook for less than 2 minutes; make sure the cheese doesn't start to bubble and leak!

10. Remove them to a paper towel–lined plate.

11. Serve immediately with warm marinara sauce.

These are yummy, crowd-pleasing little wonders!

CLASSIC HOT WINGS

Makes 4 servings

Nothing makes my husband happier than a football game. I try not to take this personally. In fact, in a desperate ploy to insert myself into his football world, I've been known to make him a batch of classic hot wings whenever a significant game is on TV. They're a little bit of a mess to make, but that just says "I love you" even more.

I think.

BLUE CHEESE DIP

1 cup mayonnaise

¾ cup sour cream

1 heaping cup blue cheese crumbles

5 to 6 dashes of Worcestershire sauce

Salt and black pepper to taste

HOT WINGS

Canola oil, for frying

24 chicken wing parts (12 wings separated into 2 pieces)

One 12-ounce bottle cayenne hot pepper sauce (such as Frank's)

½ cup (1 stick) butter

Several dashes of Worcestershire sauce

Several dashes of hot sauce (such as Tabasco)

Celery sticks, for serving

1. Begin by making a simple blue cheese dip: Combine the mayonnaise and sour cream in a bowl.

2. Stir in the crumbled blue cheese.

3. Add a few shakes of Worcestershire sauce . . .

4. And some salt and pepper. Then stir it together and store it in the fridge, covered, until the wings are ready.

5. Preheat the oven to 325°F.

6. To make the wings, heat 3 inches of canola oil in a heavy pot to 375°F. Add half the chicken wing parts to the oil . . .

7. And fry them until they're golden brown and fully cooked, about 5 minutes. Remove them and drain on paper towels, then repeat with the other half of the wing parts.

8. In a saucepan, heat the cayenne sauce and butter over medium-low heat.

9. Add the Worcestershire and Tabasco. Let it bubble up, then turn off the heat.

10. Place the wings in an ovenproof dish and pour the hot sauce all over the top. Toss to coat, then bake for 15 minutes.

11. Serve with the blue cheese dip, celery sticks . . . and your favorite cold, fizzy beverage.

Variations

- Serve with ranch dressing instead of the blue cheese dip.
- Include radishes and cucumber slices with the celery sticks.
- Make large quantities ahead of time and freeze in a large freezer bag. Reheat in a baking dish, covered in foil, in a 325°F oven.

ASIAN HOT WINGS

Makes 4 servings

Classic wings are nice and all, but I'm madly in love with this sticky, spicy version with a yummy Asian edge.
I really should have put the word "hot" in bold print, though: they'll make your brow sweat. Like, totally.

¾ cup plum jelly

¼ cup soy sauce

¼ cup rice wine vinegar

¼ cup brown sugar

2 tablespoons minced fresh ginger

1 tablespoon minced garlic

2 tablespoons minced red onion

1 tablespoon red pepper flakes
(less if you'd like less heat!)

3 to 4 assorted hot peppers
(serranos, jalapeños, chiles, and so
on), finely minced

24 chicken wing parts (12 wings
separated into 2 pieces), fried and
drained as on page 107

Thinly sliced (julienne) carrots and
cucumber, for serving

1. Preheat the oven to 325°F.

2. Add the plum jelly to a bowl.

3. Then stir in the soy sauce and rice wine vinegar.

4. Add the brown sugar, ginger, garlic, red onion, red pepper flakes, and peppers.

5. Stir to combine . . .

6. Then pour it into a saucepan and bring to a boil over medium-high heat. Reduce the heat to medium-low and cook the sauce for 15 minutes, or until slightly thickened. Turn off the heat.

7. Place the cooked wings into an ovenproof dish and pour the sauce over the top.

8. Toss the wings to coat them, then bake in the oven for 15 minutes.

9. Place the wings in dishes, then spoon extra sauce over the top.

10. Serve them with cool vegetables to go with that delicious heat. (You might want to have a glass of ice water handy, too.)

Variation

Serve with rice or noodles as a main course. Spoon extra sauce over the rice or noodles.

"We didn't start the fire."
Actually, yes we did.

Built Tim Tough.

WHISKEY-MUSTARD MEATBALLS

Makes about thirty 1-inch meatballs

These pop-in-your-mouth meatballs are perfect for any party, from the Super Bowl all the way to New Year's Eve. I can never eat just one. Or two. Or three.

Or four.

I'll stop now.

1 pound ground beef	**Salt and black pepper to taste**	**3 cups beef broth**
1 pound ground pork	**½ cup spicy mustard**	**3 tablespoons Worcestershire sauce**
1½ cup panko bread crumbs	**2 tablespoons canola oil**	**1 cup heavy cream**
1 egg	**1 cup whiskey**	

1. In a bowl, combine the beef, pork, bread crumbs, egg, salt and pepper, and ¼ cup of the spicy mustard.

2. With your hands (or a large spoon), mix the ingredients until they're well combined.

3. Use a cookie scoop or teaspoon to form balls, using your hands to shape if necessary. Place the meatballs on a cookie sheet and freeze for 10 to 15 minutes, just to firm them up.

4. Heat the canola oil in a large skillet over medium-high heat. Cook the meatballs in 3 batches, turning them to cook all over, 5 to 7 minutes to a batch. Remove the meatballs to a plate as they're done.

5. When all the meatballs are on the plate, pour the whiskey and beef broth into the skillet. Allow the mixture to bubble up and reduce for 3 to 5 minutes, or until slightly thicker.

6. Then stir in the remaining ¼ cup spicy mustard . . .

7. And the Worcestershire sauce. Stir and cook for another couple of minutes.

8. Finally, pour in the heavy cream and stir it to combine.

9. Add the browned meatballs back into the sauce.

10. Simmer for 5 to 7 minutes, or until the meatballs are cooked through.

11. Turn the skillet into a makeshift chafing dish and stick toothpicks into each meatball. Serve immediately.

Savory, spicy, and scrumptious!

Variations

- *Serve over buttered egg noodles for a main-course dish.*

- *Place in the middle of split dinner rolls to make Meatball Sliders (page 103).*

The eyes are the window to a doggie's soul.

CHERRY LIMEADE

Makes 12 to 16 servings

Cherry limeade is a summer staple where I live. It's got the nice tartness of lime and the sugary wonderfulness of bright red maraschino cherries (my youngest child's favorite part!).

I don't want to lead anyone astray, but splashing in a little vodka turns this innocent summer refreshment into a . . . well, a not-so-innocent summer refreshment. But you didn't hear that from me.

1 cup freshly squeezed lime juice
1 cup sugar

One 2-liter bottle lemon-lime soda
One 5-ounce jar maraschino cherries, with juice

Thin lime slices, for garnish

1. Begin by chilling all the ingredients thoroughly before using. Everything needs to be very cold.

2. When the ingredients are cold, add the lime juice to a pitcher or vat.

3. Add the sugar.

4. Then grab the lemon-lime soda . . .

5. And pour it right in.

6. After that, dump in a whole jar of maraschino cherries—juice and all! If you prefer the cherry limeade to be more on the light pink side, drain the cherries before adding them (and discard the juice).

7. Finally, add plenty of lime slices on top. Serve the limeade in a big, tall glass filled with ice, piling in plenty of cherries and lime slices. They're part of the treat, too!

Variations

- *Make a cherry limeade float by placing two scoops of vanilla ice cream in a large glass and pouring the limeade over the top.*

- *Spike with vodka or rum for an adult version. But only if you're an adult. Thank you for your cooperation.*

MANGO MARGARITAS

Makes 8 servings

I love anything having to do with mangoes. It sure is a good thing I live in Oklahoma!

Okay, fine. So I don't live in a tropical climate. But that's where that stuff over there on the right comes in! Jarred mango chunks are wonderful, guys. *This is not a paid advertisement.*

Make these margaritas for your friends. They're festive and fruity and fun.

2 limes

**2 tablespoons coarse sugar
(I use decorator's sugar; regular
sugar will work fine, though)**

**Two 20-ounce jars mango chunks,
drained**

1½ cups tequila

1½ cups triple sec

½ cup sugar

1. Begin by zesting the limes.

2. Then pour the coarse sugar over the lime zest and toss with your fingers to combine. Set aside.

3. Throw the mango chunks into the blender.

7. Then add ½ cup sugar . . .

11. Dip the rims of the glasses in the lime sugar.

4. Top off the blender with ice.

8. And squeeze in the juice of the limes.

12. Resist the urge to lick off the sugar and re-coat it. If I can resist it, you can too!

5. Pour in the tequila . . .

9. Blend until completely smooth, adding more ice if necessary to get it the consistency you want.

13. Pour the drinks and serve them immediately.

Hint: Freeze leftovers in a plastic storage bag. You could even pour it into a pan and make a granita out of it (see instructions on page 122).

6. And triple sec.

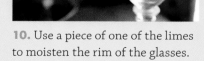

10. Use a piece of one of the limes to moisten the rim of the glasses.

And yes, I'm aware this is a martini glass. Don't be like me.

BLOODY MARY

Makes 1 large or 2 small Bloody Marys

Bloody Marys are best with that deep spicy, savory, peppery (and boozy) flavor. Here's my tasty version—both with ice and without. (Did you know a mason jar makes a really handy cocktail shaker?)

¾ cup vodka

1 or 2 limes

Montreal steak seasoning (or other steak seasoning or seasoned salt)

5 to 6 dashes of Worcestershire sauce

Dash of cayenne pepper

About 1½ cups good-quality tomato juice

Dash of salt

Dash of black pepper

Leafy celery stalk, for serving

1. Fill a standard mason jar with ice.

2. Pour in the vodka . . .

3. And squeeze in the juice of 1 or 2 limes, depending on how juicy they are.

4. Then add a few sprinkles of steak seasoning.

5. Next comes some Worcestershire sauce . . .

6. Some cayenne pepper . . .

7. And some tomato juice—pour it to the top of the jar.

8. Add a dash of salt and pepper.

9. Use a leafy celery stalk to push a squeezed lime half into the bottom of the glass, then stir everything around a bit with the celery.

Lovely!

10. If you prefer a shaken, iceless Bloody Mary, screw on the lid of the mason jar and shake it up for 20 to 30 seconds.

11. Arrange a couple of stalks of leafy celery in a glass and pour in the drink, using the lid of the mason jar as the strainer.

This right here will cure whatever ails ya.

It'll also cure whatever *doesn't* ail ya.

(I love that quality in a Bloody Mary.)

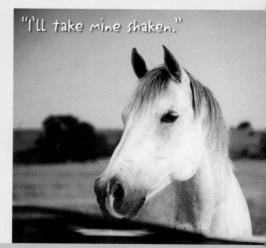

"I'll take mine shaken."

WATERMELON GRANITA

Makes 12 servings

The name *granita* is unnecessarily sophisticated; it's basically just a glorified slushie. To make granita, you do nothing more than pour a fruity liquid into a pan, then place it in the freezer and use a spoon or fork to occasionally scrape the icy mixture as it freezes. It couldn't be simpler, and there are so many different possible varieties. Just pour liquid in a pan, freeze it, and scrape it. Boom! You've just made granita. (Or maybe I should say "Brrr! You've just made a granita.")

Here's a watermelon version. The color is gorgeous, the melon flavor shines, and it just sings summer.

---

8 cups seedless watermelon chunks (about ½ watermelon)　　　**Juice of 2 limes**　　　**⅓ cup sugar**

1. Try to get your hands on a seedless watermelon. It makes things much, much easier. But a regular watermelon is just fine.

3. Cut the watermelon into wedges. Store one half in the fridge for another use.

5. Next, slice 2 limes in half and squeeze out the juice.

2. By the way, don't mess with me. I mean business. Just ask this watermelon.

4. Cut off the rind and chop the watermelon into large chunks. You can see that this "seedless" watermelon actually has a few piddly seeds. But they're light and soft—much more palatable than the big black suckers in standard watermelons.

6. Add the lime juice to a blender or food processor.

7. Add the sugar. You want to use a little, not a lot, because you want the watermelon flavor to really shine through.

8. Pack the blender as full of watermelon chunks as you can get it . . .

9. Then blend it up until it's totally pureed.

10. Pour out about half the mixture into a bowl, then add the rest of the watermelon and blend it up. If you do use a regular watermelon, you'll want to strain all of the mixture to remove the black seed particles.

"Do I want to chase that rabbit? Or do I want to stay on the porch? That is the question."

11. Pour all of the mixture into a 9 x 13-inch baking dish. Cover it with plastic wrap and freeze it for a good 2 to 3 hours for the first step.

12. Remove the pan from the fridge and gently scrape the top layer with a spoon or fork. Then, once you get close to the less frozen middle, cover the pan again (leaving the scraped portion on top of the frozen portion) and return it to the freezer for another couple of hours.

15. Serve the granita in a pretty glass, serve it in a bowl . . . or just scarf it down right out of the pan as you stand outside the freezer and try to cool down.

Not that I would ever do that, of course.

Variations

- *Use cantaloupe or honeydew chunks for a different flavor.*

- *Splash a small amount of cold wine or vodka over the granita if you're into that kind of thing.*

13. Repeat this process—freeze for a couple of hours, scrape, return to the freezer, freeze for a couple of hours, scrape, and so on. Continue until it's all scraped!

14. The great thing about granita is that the light, scraped ice on top stays perfectly frozen in the freezer. It never clumps up or crystallizes or wigs out or messes up or has an existential crisis. It's always light, cold, and perfect.

Pop Quiz: What is Cowboy Tim doing in this picture?

a) Riding a horse
b) Rounding up cattle
c) Doing what he does best
d) ALL of the above

PASTA AND PIZZA

RIGATONI AND MEATBALLS

Makes 6 to 8 servings

I always wanted to be Italian. It never materialized for me, though. Something about the fact that none of my ancestors were Italian. Details can be so annoying sometimes.

Despite my lack of Italian heritage, however, I have to say that my meatballs ain't bad at all. Marlboro Man loves them, and because long, round noodles (some humans refer to them as "spaghetti") are cumbersome and unwieldy, I take the easy road and serve mine with rigatoni.

MEATBALLS

6 thick slices crusty bread

¾ pound ground beef

¾ pound ground pork

3 garlic cloves, minced

2 eggs, beaten

¼ cup minced flat-leaf parsley, plus more for serving

¾ cup freshly grated Parmesan cheese, plus more for serving

¼ cup whole milk

¼ teaspoon salt

Freshly ground black pepper to taste

½ cup olive oil

RIGATONI AND SAUCE

1 yellow onion, diced

3 garlic cloves, minced

½ cup red wine (optional)

One 28-ounce can crushed tomatoes

One 28-ounce can whole tomatoes

¼ teaspoon salt

Freshly ground black pepper to taste

1 teaspoon sugar

¼ cup minced flat-leaf parsley

12 fresh basil leaves, cut in chiffonade (optional)

2 pounds rigatoni, cooked al dente

1. Place the bread on a baking sheet. Bake for 30 minutes in a 200°F oven, or until totally dry.

2. Break the bread into chunks . . .

3. And pulse until the bread turns into crumbs.

4. Throw the meat into a large mixing bowl.

5. Add the garlic, bread crumbs, eggs, parsley, grated Parmesan, milk, salt, and pepper. Use clean hands to mix together until well combined.

A cowboy is a cowboy, no matter what his age.

6. Use a scoop to retrieve a small amount of the meat mixture . . .

9. Remove from the pan to a plate while you make the rigatoni and sauce.

13. Whole tomatoes . . .

7. And roll it in your hands to make meatballs (about 25). Place the pan in the freezer for 10 to 15 minutes, just to firm them up.

10. Add the onion and garlic to the pan. Stir and cook for a minute or two, until the onion begins to soften.

14. Salt, pepper, and sugar . . .

8. Heat the olive oil in a heavy pot over medium-high heat. Working with 8 to 10 meatballs at a time, cook them until brown but not cooked all the way through, 2 to 3 minutes per batch.

11. Add the wine and cook for another minute. (Just omit this step if you're not using wine.)

(And yes. I drink wine from mason jars. I am not ashamed.)

15. And parsley and basil.

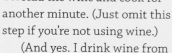

12. Add the crushed tomatoes . . .

16. Stir the sauce to combine all the ingredients . . . Cover and reduce the heat to a simmer. Cook for 30 minutes, stirring occasionally.

17. Then throw in the meat-a-balls!

18. Stir gently, then cover and cook for 20 more minutes, stirring once or twice, until the meatballs are cooked through.

"Happiness is a boy and his football." —Confucius

19. Heap the rigatoni on a large platter and pile the meatballs and sauce on the top. Sprinkle on some extra minced parsley and serve with extra grated Parmesan.

This is a good one, my friends.

I mean . . . *i miei amici.*

Sincerely,
Costanza

Variations

- Use leftover meatballs to make Meatball Sliders (page 103).
- Slice leftover meatballs and use as a pizza topping.

CHICKEN PARMESAN

6 servings

This classic, hearty, bountiful, abundant, delicious (do we have enough adjectives yet?) Italian classic is a favorite in my household, all the way from my youngest son to the man I done got hitched to. It's been inducted into the Hall of Fame in my kitchen.

I can prove it. I have a plaque.

½ **cup all-purpose flour**

½ **teaspoon salt, plus more to taste**

½ **teaspoon black pepper, plus more to taste**

6 **boneless, skinless chicken breasts, pounded to uniform thinness**

2 **tablespoons butter**

½ **cup olive oil**

1 **medium onion, chopped**

4 **garlic cloves, minced**

¾ **cup wine (white or red is fine)**

Three **14.5-ounce cans crushed tomatoes**

2 **tablespoons sugar**

¼ **cup chopped fresh parsley, plus more for sprinkling**

1½ **cups freshly grated Parmesan cheese**

1 **pound thin linguine or other pasta, cooked al dente**

1. Mix the flour and salt and pepper on a large plate.

2. Season the flattened chicken breasts on both sides with salt and pepper, then dredge them in the flour mixture.

3. Set them aside.

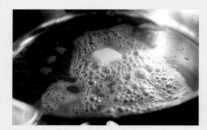

4. In a large skillet over medium-high heat, melt the butter in the olive oil until sizzling.

5. Fry the chicken breasts until nice and golden brown, 2 to 3 minutes per side. Remove the chicken from the skillet and keep warm.

6. Without cleaning the skillet, add the onion and garlic and sauté for 2 minutes, or until the onion starts to brown.

7. Pour in the wine and scrape the bottom of the pan, getting all the flavorful bits off the bottom. Allow the wine to cook down until reduced by half, about 3 minutes.

8. Pour in the crushed tomatoes and stir to combine.

9. Add the sugar, then add salt and pepper to taste. Stir, reduce the heat to low, and simmer for 30 minutes so the flavors can meld.

10. Add the chopped parsley . . .

11. And ½ cup of the grated Parmesan, then stir to combine.

12. Carefully lay the chicken breasts on top of the sauce and completely cover them with the remaining 1 cup grated Parmesan.

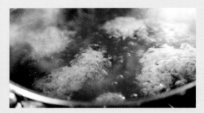

13. Cover the skillet and simmer until the cheese is melted and the chicken is heated through, about 5 minutes.

14. Place the cooked pasta in pasta bowls or on plates, then cover it with sauce. Lay a chicken breast on top of each serving and sprinkle with more parsley.
Serve immediately. Yum!

FANCY MAC AND CHEESE

Makes 12 servings

This is one of those recipes that can definitely be described as ridiculous, where *ridiculous* means so decadent, delicious, and divine that it almost renders the person eating it speechless. A little goes a long way with this one. Invite lots of guests . . . preferably guests you really, really like!

16 ounces white button or cremini mushrooms, quartered

Olive oil, for drizzling

Kosher salt and black pepper to taste

8 slices thick-cut bacon

2 yellow onions, peeled, halved, and thinly sliced

5 tablespoons butter, plus more for buttering the pan

½ cup grated Parmesan cheese

½ cup grated Gruyère cheese

½ cup grated fontina cheese

4 ounces goat cheese (chèvre)

1½ pounds macaroni

¼ cup all-purpose flour

2 cups whole milk

½ cup half-and-half

2 eggs, beaten

4 ounces crumbled Gorgonzola or other blue cheese

1. Preheat the oven to 425°F.

2. Drizzle the mushrooms with olive oil, then sprinkle them with salt and pepper.

3. Roast them in the oven until deep golden brown, 20 to 25 minutes. Set aside. Try not to eat them before the macaroni's done.

4. Next, fry thick slices of bacon until chewy but not yet crisp.

5. Chop up the bacon into bite-size bits. Set aside. Try not to eat them before the macaroni's done.

6. In a large skillet over medium-low heat, sauté the onions in 1 tablespoon butter, stirring occasionally, until golden brown, about 15 minutes. Set aside. Try not to . . . oh, never mind.

7. Grate the Parmesan, Gruyère, and fontina cheeses. Unwrap the goat cheese.

8. Cook the macaroni until just undercooked. Set aside.

9. To make the sauce, melt the remaining 4 tablespoons butter in a large pot over medium heat.

10. Sprinkle in the flour, whisking to combine.

Bringing in the sheaves. I mean calves.

11. Let the roux cook for a minute or so, whisking constantly.

15. And ½ teaspoon pepper.

19. Stir until the cheeses melt.

12. Then pour in the milk, whisking constantly. Cook the white sauce for 3 to 5 minutes, or until thick and bubbly.

16. Spoon some of the hot sauce into the beaten eggs to temper them, stirring with a fork to incorporate the mixture without cooking the eggs.

20. Add the cooked macaroni and stir to coat. Splash in a little milk or hot water if needed for thinning.

13. Next, add the half-and-half . . .

17. Pour the tempered eggs into the white sauce, stirring constantly as you add them.

21. Preheat the oven to 350°F and butter a 9 x 13-inch baking pan.

14. 1 teaspoon salt . . .
  (Freaky pink alien claw alert!)

18. Add the Parmesan, Gruyère, fontina, and goat cheeses.

22. Lay on half the onions . . .

23. Half the macaroni . . .

25. Half the Gorgonzola . . .

24. Half the mushrooms . . .

26. And half the bacon.

27. Repeat the layers, ending with the bacon. Bake for 20 to 25 minutes, or until bubbly and hot.

This is the stuff that dreams—and love handles—are made of.

Variations

- *Substitute diced ham or pancetta for the bacon.*
- *Use different cheeses to your liking.*
- *Serve with steak or chicken as a side dish, or with a green salad as a main dish.*

PASTA WITH PESTO CREAM SAUCE

Makes 6 to 8 servings

Fresh basil is one of those things I consider a real treasure, because I'm not able to have it at my fingertips year-round. I usually can't get fresh herbs at my small-town grocery store, so during the winter when I can't grow them myself, I'm pretty much wandering in an herbless wilderness. But during the summer, when my garden is bulging with basil plants, I make fresh pesto as often as I can. It's almost become a condiment: I add it to pasta, quiches, scrambled eggs . . . and I mix it with mayonnaise for a splendid sandwich spread.

One of my favorite uses for basil is to stir it into warm cream and pour it over cooked pasta. You can't know the beauty until you try it.

¾ cup fresh basil leaves

¾ cup grated Parmesan cheese

3 tablespoons pine nuts

2 garlic cloves, peeled

Salt and black pepper

⅓ cup extra-virgin olive oil, a little more if needed

½ cup heavy cream

2 tablespoons butter

12 ounces pasta, such as fusilli or cavatappi, cooked to al dente

4 roma tomatoes, diced

1. First, make the pesto: Add the basil to a food processor or blender.

4. Peeled garlic cloves . . .

7. Stop when it's beautiful and bright green and all mixed together nicely.

2. Add ½ cup of the grated Parmesan . . .

5. And salt and pepper to taste.

8. Now comes the even better part: Heat the heavy cream in a saucepan and drop in a couple of tablespoons of butter.

3. The pine nuts . . .

6. Next, turn on the machine and slowly drizzle in the olive oil to make a nice puree.

9. Then pour the pesto right in.

10. This is art, I tell you! Gorgeous, fragrant, fattening, luscious art.

11. Stir this together and just simmer it slowly for a few minutes.

12. At the end, dump in the remaining ¼ cup grated Parmesan and stir it together.

13. Drain the pasta and put it in a large serving bowl.

14. Pour on the pesto cream . . .

15. Then throw in the diced tomatoes.

16. Toss it all together and serve it right away. The hot pasta and sauce will heat the tomatoes just perfectly.

This is positively divine. One of my favorite things.

Variations

· *Serve with grilled shrimp or chicken.*

· *Stir 4 ounces goat cheese (chèvre) into the cream mixture for a nice tangy flavor.*

PESTO

· Mix with softened cream cheese for a cracker spread.

· Mix with mayo for a yummy sandwich spread.

· Stir into the quiche mixtures before baking (see pages 32 and 34).

· Spread on an unbaked pizza crust before adding toppings.

· Freeze in an ice-cube tray, then drop individual cubes into pasta sauces and soups for added flavor.

PASTA WITH TOMATO CREAM SAUCE

Makes 6 to 8 servings

My love for pasta is well established. My love for pasta with tomato cream sauce is *weller* established. I mean well established*er*. I mean *more well established*.

Never mind. Goodness gracious.

Tomato cream sauce is my life: the tang of tomato and the rich sinfulness of cream. This pasta is equally delicious on its own (for me) or next to a juicy steak (for my husband). Try it within the next five minutes! It's really that good.

12 ounces fettuccine or other pasta

2 tablespoons olive oil

2 tablespoons butter

1 medium onion, finely diced

4 garlic cloves, minced

Two 15-ounce cans tomato sauce or marinara sauce

Salt and black pepper to taste

Dash of sugar, or more to taste

1 cup heavy cream

½ cup grated Parmesan or Romano cheese, or more to taste

Chopped fresh basil

1. Cook the fettuccine according to package directions, reserving a little hot pasta water for later.

2. Heat the olive oil and butter in a large skillet over medium heat. Add the onion and garlic and sauté until the onion is translucent, about 4 minutes.

3. Pour in the tomato sauce. Add the salt, pepper, and sugar, then stir it around and cook until warm.

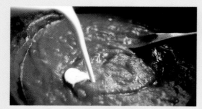

4. Next comes the heavy cream. Go ahead. Everybody's doing it.

5. Stir in the cream . . .

6. And watch it slowly turn from a red-and-white mess to a light orange pan of heaven.

7. Now drain the pasta . . .

8. Dump some grated Parmesan into the sauce . . .

9. And dump the hot pasta right on top.

10. Toss the pasta and sauce together and splash in some hot pasta water if the sauce is too thick.

11. Just before serving, toss in a little more Parmesan and chopped fresh basil.

12. Serve it immediately.

Variations

- Stir a couple of tablespoons of Pesto (page 137) into the sauce.

- Serve with grilled chicken, fish, or steak.

PIZZA DOUGH

Makes enough dough for 1 pizza

This is my favorite pizza crust, and I've used it for years and years. So simple, so flavorful, so foolproof!
You can double or triple the recipe to make as many pizzas as you'd like.

1 scant teaspoon active dry yeast

¾ cup warm water

2 cups all-purpose flour

¾ teaspoon kosher salt

3 tablespoons olive oil

1. Combine the yeast and warm water in a small bowl. Allow it to sit for 10 minutes.

3. Sprinkle in the salt.

5. Finally, pour in the yeast/water mixture.

2. Add the flour to the bowl of an electric mixer fitted with the paddle attachment.

4. Turn the mixer on low, then slowly pour in the olive oil.

6. Stop mixing when everything comes together. Transfer to a lightly oiled bowl and cover with plastic wrap. Allow the dough to rise 1 hour before using.

The dough can be stored in the fridge for several days before using.

The dough recipe may be doubled or tripled depending on the quantity you need.

STEAKHOUSE PIZZA

Makes 8 to 10 servings

Warning: If you make this for a dude, he will love you forever. So make sure the dude is someone you don't mind loving you forever. Otherwise it could be a little inconvenient.

1 skirt steak or flank steak, 1½ to 2 pounds

Salt and black pepper to taste

2 red onions, halved and thinly sliced

1 tablespoon olive oil, plus more for drizzling

4 tablespoons balsamic vinegar

2 cups good marinara sauce (store-bought is just fine)

1 recipe Pizza Dough (page 141)

12 ounces fresh mozzarella cheese, thinly sliced

Steak sauce to taste

Shaved Parmesan cheese

1. Preheat the oven to 500°F and arrange the oven rack to the very bottom position.

2. Season the steak with salt and pepper. Truth be told, you could put this on a plate in front of some dudes and just call it dinner.
　　Man like meat.

3. Grill both sides of the steak over medium heat until medium rare, just about 2 minutes per side. You want the steak to be nice and pinkish red in the middle, so don't overdo it!

5. In a large skillet over medium heat, sauté the red onion slices in 1 tablespoon olive oil and 2 tablespoons balsamic vinegar until soft, about 10 minutes.

6. Mix the marinara sauce with the remaining 2 tablespoons balsamic vinegar.

4. Remove it from the heat and set it aside.

Blessed are the peacemakers.

7. Roll out the pizza dough into a large oval and place it on a baking sheet.

8. Spread the sauce mixture all over the surface of the crust.

9. Arrange the onion slices all over the sauce.

10. Lay the mozzarella slices over the onions, then place the pan in the oven on the lower rack. Bake for 12 to 15 minutes, or until the crust is golden and the cheese is bubbly and hot.

11. While the pizza is baking, slice the grilled steak very thin.

12. Pull the pizza from the oven and immediately lay the steak slices over the top.

13. Transfer the pizza to a cutting board.

14. Then grab some steak sauce . . .

15. And drizzle it all over the steak.

16. Sprinkle with the Parmesan shavings, then serve it with a big, green salad. You and whatever dude's sitting at the table with you (which, if you're a dude, might actually be you. Never mind. This is getting philosophically and existentially confusing.) will love every wonderful bite.

Variations

- *Sprinkle with sliced green onions.*
- *Substitute blue cheese crumbles for the Parmesan shavings.*

THAI CHICKEN PIZZA

Makes 8 to 10 servings

This is a lovely, fresh, Asian-inspired pizza that's really different and unexpected. I'd eat it weekly if I could!

Wait. I can. So why don't I? I'll have to think about that for a while.

2 garlic cloves, peeled

2 tablespoons minced fresh ginger

¼ cup soy sauce

3 teaspoons sesame oil

½ teaspoon fish sauce

1½ cups smooth peanut butter

½ cup very warm water

4 tablespoons Thai chili paste (sold in the Asian foods aisle)

2 boneless, skinless chicken breasts

Salt and black pepper to taste

1 recipe Pizza Dough (page 141)

Olive oil, for drizzling

4 tablespoons Thai sweet chili sauce

12 ounces fresh mozzarella, thinly sliced

1 cup alfalfa or bean sprouts

2 cups shredded carrots

2 cups cilantro leaves

½ cup chopped peanuts

1. Preheat the oven to 500°F and arrange the oven rack at the lowest position.

2. First, make the peanut sauce: To the bowl of a food processor or blender, add the garlic and ginger . . .

3. Soy sauce . . .

4. Sesame oil . . .

5. And fish sauce, which is quite salty and stinky.

6. Next, add the peanut butter . . .

7. And the water. Blend as you're pouring it in.

8. Check the consistency, give it a taste, and add a little more of whatever it needs! Add more warm water if it needs thinning.

9. Oh! I forgot to add some chili paste. I added a little, then tasted . . . then added more. I like it hot!

10. Next, sprinkle the chicken breasts with salt and pepper, and grill them on both sides until done. Remove from the grill and slice thin. (You can also sauté them in a skillet if you prefer.)

(Also, you just need 2 breasts for this recipe. As usual, I'm cooking up some extras.)

11. To assemble the pizza, roll out the dough and place onto a baking pan drizzled with olive oil. Spread 4 tablespoons sweet chili sauce all over the dough.

12. Lay on the mozzarella slices, then the chicken slices.

14. Throw on as many sprouts as you'd like.

15. Next, add the shredded carrots and cilantro leaves.

17. End with a sprinkling of chopped peanuts.

This one's mine. Where's yours?

Okay, fine. I guess you can have a bite or two.

13. Bake for 12 to 15 minutes, or until the crust is golden and the cheese is bubbly.

16. Drizzle the peanut sauce all over the top of the pizza.

Variations

- Save extra peanut sauce for another use: Stir it into an Asian chicken salad, use it as a dipping sauce for chicken strips, and so on.

- You can use store-bought peanut/satay sauce to save a few steps.

Sunrise on a ranch = The closest thing to Heaven that you'll ever see.

FIG-PROSCIUTTO PIZZA

Makes 8 to 10 servings

The beauty of this pizza is the combination of the sweet fig spread and the salty, flavorful prosciutto. The piled-on-high layer of spicy arugula gives this pizza an indescribable (and highly addictive) flavor.

1 recipe Pizza Dough (page 141)

½ cup fig spread or fig preserves

Kosher salt

12 ounces fresh mozzarella, thinly sliced

8 ounces prosciutto, thinly sliced

12 ounces arugula

Shaved Parmesan cheese (optional)

1. Preheat the oven to 500°F and arrange the oven rack on the lowest position.

2. Roll out the pizza dough as thin as it'll go. Pour on the fig spread . . .

3. Then spread it thinly all over the surface of the dough. Sprinkle it lightly with kosher salt.

4. Lay the mozzarella slices all over the top of the spread.

5. Bake for 12 to 15 minutes, until the crust is golden brown and the cheese is melted and bubbly.

6. Drape the prosciutto slices all over the hot pizza. This'll allow them to get nice and warm without becoming crisp and sizzling in the oven.

7. Pile on the arugula as high as you want it to go . . .

8. Then sprinkle on some Parmesan shavings if you'd like.

CARNITAS PIZZA

Makes 8 to 10 servings

I love carnitas. I love pizza. Ergo, I love carnitas pizza!

I've always loved mathematics. (Or is it logic? Or is it statistics?)

Oh, well. Let's just make the pizza and figure it out later.

2 teaspoons chili powder

1 teaspoon ground cumin

1 teaspoon dried oregano

1 teaspoon kosher salt

One 3- or 4-pound chuck roast

2 tablespoons canola oil

Two 12-ounce cans pineapple, papaya, or mango juice

1 recipe Pizza Dough (page 141)

Olive oil, for drizzling

1 cup jarred tomatillo salsa, plus more for serving

12 ounces fresh mozzarella, thinly sliced

1 yellow onion, thinly sliced and sautéed until golden

1 red bell pepper, thinly sliced and sautéed until golden

3 green onions, sliced

Sour cream, for serving (optional)

Guacamole, for serving (optional)

Laugh and my brother-in-law Tim laughs with you!

1. Preheat the oven to 300°F.

2. Mix the chili powder, cumin, oregano, and salt.

3. Rub the spice mixture on both sides of the roast.

4. Heat the canola oil in a large pot over high heat, then sear both sides of the roast until nice and brown, about 2 minutes per side.

5. Grab the juice. Any kind will work! (This is technically "nectar" and it works fine, too.)

6. Pour the juice into the pot with the meat. Cover and roast for about 4 hours, or until the meat is falling apart. Use 2 forks to shred the meat, then return it to the cooking liquid to keep it warm.

7. Increase the oven's heat to 500°F.

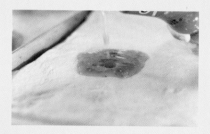

8. Roll out the pizza dough into a rectangle, as thin as it will go. Drizzle a baking sheet with olive oil and transfer the dough to the baking sheet. Pour on the tomatillo salsa, then spread it thinly all over the surface of the dough.

9. Lay the mozzarella slices all over the top, then add the yellow onion and pepper.

10. Bake the pizza for 12 to 15 minutes, or until the crust is golden brown and the cheese is bubbly.

11. Lay the warm shredded meat over the top. Be sure to get plenty of the juices on there! It'll make the pizza extra delicious.

12. Then sprinkle with the sliced green onions, slice into pieces, and serve to hungry humanoids with little dishes of extra tomatillo salsa. Sour cream and guacamole are good, too!

Variations

- *Substitute beef broth for the fruit juice if you prefer a more savory flavor.*
- *Sprinkle fresh chopped jalapeños over the baked pizza.*

SUPPER

BARBECUE CHICKEN AND PINEAPPLE QUESADILLAS

Makes 4 quesadillas

I have a slight problem when it comes to quesadillas, and that is that I pretty much want to eat them all the time. *All the, all the, all the time.* It was my number one craving during all four of my pregnancies, and there's no limit to the different combinations and permutations of fillings I'll try.

½ pineapple

Salt and black pepper to taste

2 boneless, skinless chicken breasts, pounded to uniform thickness with a mallet

⅓ cup barbecue sauce

4 tablespoons butter, for frying

8 small flour or corn tortillas

1 jalapeño, sliced

1½ cups grated Monterey Jack cheese

Sour cream, for serving

Pico de gallo or salsa, for serving

1. Soak 8 wooden skewers in water for at least 1 hour.

2. Cut the pineapple into 8 wedges . . .

3. And cut off the hard core and the outer skin.

4. Thread the pieces of pineapple onto the wooden skewers . . .

5. And grill over medium-high heat, turning once or twice during the grilling process.

6. Remove the pineapple from the grill and slice it into chunks. Set aside.

7. Salt and pepper the flattened chicken breasts, then grill or sauté them over medium-high heat until done, about 4 minutes per side. Brush both sides generously with barbecue sauce . . .

8. Then remove them from the grill and slice them thinly.

9. Now assemble the quesadillas: On top of 1 tortilla, place some chicken, some pineapple chunks, and some sliced jalapeño.

10. Drizzle barbecue sauce all over the ingredients . . .

11. Then cover it all with grated cheese.

12. Heat 1 tablespoon butter in a large skillet. Top the quesadilla with the second tortilla. Brown on one side, then carefully flip the quesadilla and brown the other side. Make sure all the cheese is melted! Repeat to make the rest of the quesadillas.

13. Slice the quesadillas into wedges . . .

14. Then serve them with sour cream, pico de gallo, and a wedge of grilled pineapple on top.

Variations

- *Serve with Mexican Rice (page 173) and other side dishes as shown with Tequila Lime Chicken (page 170).*

- *Serve with Restaurant-Style Salsa (page 92).*

- *Serve grilled pineapple on its own as a snack or side dish.*

QUESADILLAS DE CAMARONES

Makes 6 quesadillas

What can I say? I'm addicted to quesadillas, and there are few things I won't put inside them. Except maybe Oreos.

Wait. Now *there's* an idea . . .

2 tablespoons olive oil

2 pounds large shrimp, peeled and deveined, tails off

Salt to taste

7 ounces Mexican tomato sauce (see page 66) or enchilada sauce

1 large onion, cut in half and then into slices

1 red bell pepper, seeded and sliced into strips

1 green bell pepper, seeded and sliced into strips

6 tablespooons butter, for frying

12 large flour tortillas

2½ cups grated cheese (Monterey Jack is best)

Pico de gallo, for serving

Guacamole, for serving

1. Heat 1 tablespoon olive oil in a large skillet over high heat. Throw in the shrimp.

2. Toss around and cook until the shrimp are opaque, about 5 minutes. Sprinkle with salt and reduce the heat to low.

3. Pour in the tomato sauce.

4. Stir around and allow to simmer for a couple of minutes.

5. Remove the shrimp from the skillet . . .

6. And chop it into chunks. Set these aside for a bit.

7. In a separate skillet, heat the remaining 1 tablespoon olive oil over high heat. Throw in the onion and peppers and cook for 3 to 4 minutes, or until the peppers have a few dark brown/black areas.

8. Remove the peppers from the skillet and set them aside.

9. Sizzle ½ tablespoon butter in a skillet over medium heat and lay a flour tortilla in the pan. Cover with grated cheese.

10. Cover the cheese with peppers . . .

11. And lay the chopped shrimp on top of the peppers. When the tortilla is golden, top with a second tortilla and carefully flip the quesadilla to the other side, adding the other ½ tablespoon butter to the skillet at the same time. Continue cooking until the second side is golden. Repeat with the remaining tortillas and fillings.

12. Cut each quesadilla into wedges and serve with pico de gallo and guacamole.

Variations

- *Use smaller tortillas for appetizer-sized quesadilla wedges.*

- *Substitute diced chicken breasts for the shrimp: cook until done, then add the red sauce.*

- *Use corn tortillas for a slightly different flavor and texture.*

SPICY DR PEPPER PULLED PORK

12 servings

Oh, boy, is this good. And spicy! Put it on a sandwich. Throw it into tacos. Eat it by itself. Either way, have a cool cloth and an ice bath nearby. It'll clear your sinuses in the most wonderful way.

2 onions, peeled and quartered

**1 whole pork butt
(pork shoulder roast)**

Salt and black pepper to taste

**One 11-ounce can chipotle chiles
in adobo sauce**

Two 12-ounce cans Dr Pepper

**4 tablespoons packed brown
sugar**

1. Preheat the oven to 300°F.

2. Start by placing the onion quarters in the bottom of a pot.

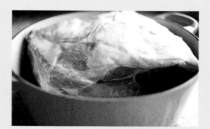

3. Place the pork butt on top of the onions and add salt and pepper to taste.

4. Pour the chipotle chiles over the top.

5. Crack open a couple of cans of the hard stuff . . .

6. And pour them over the chiles. Add the brown sugar to the liquid, stirring slightly to combine.

7. Cover the pot and cook for at least 6 hours, flipping the roast 2 to 3 times during the cooking process. When it's done, it'll be dark and weird and wonderful.

8. It'll also be fork-tender. That's when you know it's ready. (If the pork does not easily pull apart with forks, return it to the oven in 30-minute intervals until done.)

9. Remove the roast from the pot and shred it completely.

10. Spoon the fat from the top of the liquid in the pot. Then return the meat to the pot and keep it in the juice until you need it. Divine!

Variations

- Pile it on a toasted deli roll.
- Pile it on nachos.
- Use it to fill tacos or quesadillas.
- Use it as a pizza topping.
- Serve it as is with mashed potatoes, Twice-Baked New Potatoes (page 212), buttered egg noodles, Grits (page 200), or Panfried Kale (page 214).

Hay meadow? Or Hades? Sometimes it's hard to tell.

HIS/HER BURGERS

Makes 8 to 10 burgers

Burger time is just another time to conduct a Battle of the Sexes competition in my world.

Boys = bacon, cheese, and spice

Girls = anything, because we women are, like, soooo adaptable

I love my burgers piled high, and I don't care with what. Gimme mushrooms, gimme cheese, gimme caramelized onions. As long as I can open my mouth wide enough to eat it, I'm good.

HIS BURGERS

2 chipotle peppers in adobo sauce

¼ cup mayonnaise

4 slices bacon, cooked and halved

2 thick slices Cheddar cheese

8 jarred jalapeño slices

HER BURGERS

¼ cup mayonnaise

1 tablespoon Pesto (page 137 or store-bought)

1 medium red onion, sliced and sautéed in 1 tablespoon butter until golden brown

8 ounces button mushrooms, sautéed in 1 tablespoon butter until golden brown

½ cup crumbled blue cheese

MEAT MIXTURE

2 pounds 80/20 ground beef

1 teaspoon salt

½ teaspoon black pepper

⅓ cup heavy cream

5 dashes of Worcestershire sauce

Tabasco sauce to taste

8 to 10 burger buns

1. For His burgers, chop the chipotle peppers.

2. Place them into a dish with the mayonnaise . . .

3. And stir to combine. Set aside.

4. For Her burgers, place the mayonnaise and pesto in a bowl . . .

5. And stir to combine. Set aside.

6. For the meat mixture, add the meat, salt, and pepper to a bowl.

7. Add the cream, Worcestershire sauce, and Tabasco. Mix together until well combined.

8. Form into 8 to 10 patties.

9. Grill them (or fry them in a skillet over medium-high heat) until they're no longer pink in the middle.

10. To build His burgers, top each patty with bacon and melt the cheese on top. Top with the jalapeño slices and spread the top and bottom bun with a generous amount of chipotle mayonnaise.

11. To build Her burgers, spread both sides of the bun with the pesto mayo. Top the patty with caramelized red onion, sautéed mushrooms, and crumbled blue cheese.

Variations

• *Boys may eat Her burgers.*

• *Girls may eat His burgers.*

• *To do away with gender stereotypes altogether, you may put all of the ingredients on one burger and just call it a day.*

OTHER YUMMY TOPPINGS

Avocado slices, pico de gallo, Restaurant-Style Salsa (page 92), Sweet Lime Pickles (page 280), Pepper Jack cheese

FRIED CHICKEN TACOS

Makes 16 tacos, 8 servings

These are the best chicken tacos in the world. My brother's been making them since his college days, and while they're a mess and a half to make, they're also lots of fun if you have a little help.

Hot oil alert! Please be careful: Keep the skillet on the back burner to protect little kiddoes.

1 teaspoon chili powder

1 teaspoon ground cumin

½ teaspoon salt

1 cup plus 1 tablespoon canola oil

1½ pounds boneless, skinless chicken breasts, cut into small cubes

Two 4-ounce cans diced green chiles

16 small corn tortillas

1½ cups finely grated cheese (Cheddar or Cheddar-Jack blend)

Sour cream

Hot sauce, such as Cholula

2 cups thinly sliced romaine (or other) lettuce

4 roma tomatoes, diced

1. Mix the chili powder, cumin, and salt together in a small bowl. Set aside.

2. Heat 1 tablespoon of the canola oil in a large skillet over medium-high heat. Add the chicken and chiles and sauté for 3 to 4 minutes, or until the chicken has lost its color.

3. Sprinkle the spice mixture over the chicken and sauté until the chicken is cooked through. Remove the pan from the heat and set aside.

4. In a separate skillet, heat 1 cup of the canola oil over medium-high heat. Drop in a small piece of tortilla to see if it's hot enough; it should sizzle as soon as it hits the oil.

5. Spoon about ¼ cup of the chicken into a tortilla.

6. Grasp the tortilla closed between tongs . . .

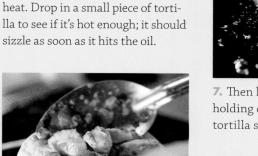

7. Then lay it in the hot oil, holding down the top half of the tortilla so that it remains closed.

8. Cook until golden brown, 30 to 45 seconds, then flip the tacos over to fry the other side.

9. And cook the other side until browned and crispy.

This is how my nephew looks at me whenever I yell across the pasture, "CALEB! HI! OVER HERE! LOOK AT AUNT REE! SMILE!" He loves me.

10. Remove each taco from the pan, allowing the excess oil to drip out of one end.

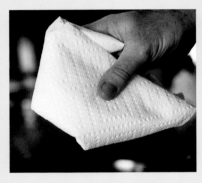

11. Immediately wrap each taco in a paper towel and gently shake it to remove any excess oil.

(This is my brother's big, hairy hand, by the way. It was important for me to point that out to you.)

12. While the tacos are still hot, gently stick some cheese inside.

13. Next, using a knife, smear some sour cream on top of the cheese . . .

14. And drizzle hot sauce on top of the sour cream.

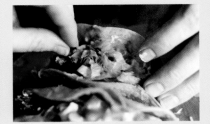

15. Next come shredded lettuce and tomatoes. It helps to have an assembly line!

This is what chicken tacos are meant to be. It is their destiny.

Variations

- *Serve with Restaurant-Style Salsa (page 92) and Grilled Corn Guacamole (page 90).*

- *Mango Margaritas (page 116) would be the perfect accompaniment.*

- *Serve with any of the side dishes shown with Tequila Lime Chicken (page 170).*

Our love for KittenKitten knows no bounds.

BEEF STEW

Makes 8 servings

Average beef stew is . . . well, average. But good beef stew is out of this world, as evidenced by the joy you'll experience while chowing down on this dang delicious version.

3 tablespoons olive oil

1 tablespoon butter

2 pounds beef stew meat

1 medium onion, diced

3 garlic cloves, minced

1 can or bottle of beer

4 cups beef broth

1 tablespoon Worcestershire sauce

2 tablespoons tomato paste

½ teaspoon paprika

1½ teaspoons sugar

½ teaspoon kosher salt

Freshly ground black pepper

4 new potatoes, quartered

4 carrots, unpeeled, roughly sliced

2 tablespoons all-purpose flour

Minced parsley, for garnish (optional)

Crusty bread, for serving

1. Start by heating the olive oil and butter in a large pot or Dutch oven over medium-high heat. Throw in the stew meat and quickly brown it on all sides, about 5 minutes.

3. Throw the onion into the pot, then reduce the heat to low.

5. Then throw in the garlic and stir it around to cook for a minute.

2. Remove the meat to a clean plate and set aside.

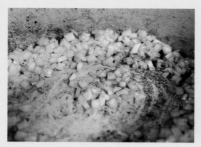

4. Stir the onion around to cook until softened, about 3 minutes . . .

6. Pour in the beer . . .

7. Beef broth . . .

8. Worcestershire sauce . . .

9. Tomato paste . . .

10. Paprika . . .

11. Sugar, salt, and pepper.

12. Finally, return the meat to the pot, cover it, and simmer the stew over very low heat for 1½ to 2 hours, or until the meat is very tender. If the liquid level gets too low, add 1 to 2 cups hot water as needed.

13. Add the potatoes and carrots to the pot. Stir them in and continue simmering for 30 minutes more, or until the vegetables are tender.

14. To thicken the stew, remove 1 cup of the cooking liquid and whisk in the flour.

15. Pour the flour mixture into the pot and simmer for an additional 10 minutes, or until the stew is very thick. Add parsley at the end if desired.

16. Dish it up and serve it with crusty bread and a very, very hearty appetite.

Variations

- Serve the stew with Twice-Baked New Potatoes (page 212) or on top of Grits (page 200).

- Place leftover stew in a baking dish and top with puff pastry or pie crust to make beef pot pie.

- Stew freezes beautifully!

SHEPHERD'S PIE

Makes 1 pie; size varies depending on how much stew you use

My beef stew freezes so nicely that sometimes I double the recipe so I'll have extra on hand. And extra beef stew cries out to be turned into shepherd's pie. It's so easy, and so comforting and wonderful. Make it in a large dish or skillet, or even in individual ramekins!

At least 4 cups leftover Beef Stew (page 165)

Mashed potatoes, whatever amount you need to cover the stew (your favorite recipe)

Minced parsley, for garnish

1. Preheat the oven to 375°F.

2. Place the leftover stew in an ovenproof skillet or baking dish. I had a whole recipe of stew, so I went for the big guns and used it all.

3. Spoon mashed potatoes all over the surface of the stew . . .

4. Then use a spoon or spatula to spread them out. If you'd like to be fancy and pipe a decorative pattern with the potatoes, knock yourself out. But this ain't that kind of operation.

5. Then just put the skillet into the oven and bake it until the top is nice and golden brown—I even like to go a little overboard and get some crusty parts going. The mashed potatoes below remain nice and soft, so it makes for a lot of different textures. Sprinkle on a little minced parsley when you remove it from the oven.

6. Dish it up with a large spoon.

To die for. Just to die for. Your family will love it.

And, most important, so will you!

I Heart Herefords. Not to be confused with heifers. See page 35.

TEQUILA LIME CHICKEN

Makes 6 servings

I love big platters of Mexican food with all sorts of different things going on. The star of this show is a flavorful sliced chicken breast marinated in lime and tequila, then grilled to perfection and topped with fresh pico de gallo. It's perfectly delicious by itself, but on a plate with refried black beans, rice, and warm tortillas? It's a regular fiesta . . . right on your dining room table.

3 limes

5 garlic cloves, peeled

1 jalapeño, sliced

1 teaspoon kosher salt

½ cup chopped cilantro

5 tablespoons olive oil

¾ cup tequila

6 boneless, skinless chicken breasts

OPTIONAL FOR SERVING

Pico de gallo

Jalapeño slices

Refried black beans (heat two 14.5-ounce cans of black beans in a saucepan, then mash slightly)

Mexican Rice (page 173)

Warmed flour or corn tortillas

Lime wedges

Avocado slices

Sour cream

Grated Monterey Jack cheese

1. Slice open the limes . . .

3. Jalapeño slices . . .

5. Cilantro . . .

2. And squeeze the juice into a food processor or blender. Add the garlic cloves . . .

4. Kosher salt . . .

6. Olive oil . . .

7. And tequila.

8. Blend the mixture until totally pureed . . .

9. Then add the chicken breasts to a large plastic bag and pour in the marinade. Seal the bag and marinate in the fridge for several hours or overnight.

10. Remove the chicken from the bag and grill it over medium-high heat.

11. Rotate the chicken 45 degrees on both sides to create nice grill marks, and continue grilling until the chicken is cooked thoroughly, 4 to 5 minutes per side.

12. Slice the chicken and serve it on a plate topped with pico de gallo and a jalapeño slice, surrounded by refried black beans, Mexican Rice (page 173), rolled-up warm tortillas, and a couple of lime wedges. You can also add some avocado slices, some sour cream . . . go ahead and load it up!

(You can also melt some Monterey Jack cheese over the top of the sliced chicken breast. Yummy.)

Variations

- *Use the marinade for shrimp.*
- *Serve with Mango Margaritas (page 116)!*

Professor Walter!

MEXICAN RICE

Makes 6 servings

Just a good, basic side dish to go with all your Tex-Mex delights.

2 tablespoons canola oil

1 large onion, chopped

3 garlic cloves, minced

2 cups long-grain rice

One 10-ounce can Rotel Diced Tomatoes and Green Chiles

One 14.5-ounce can whole tomatoes

1 teaspoon ground cumin, or more to taste

¼ teaspoon cayenne pepper

1 teaspoon kosher salt

2 to 3 cups low-sodium chicken broth

Chopped fresh cilantro, for garnish

Heat the oil in a large skillet over medium-high heat. Add the onion and garlic and cook for 3 to 4 minutes. Reduce the heat to low and add the rice. Cook over low heat for 3 minutes, stirring constantly to make sure the rice doesn't burn. Add the Rotel, whole tomatoes, cumin, cayenne, and salt. Stir to combine and cook for 2 minutes. Add 2 cups of the broth and bring to a boil. Reduce the heat to low, cover, and simmer for 10 to 15 minutes more, or until the rice is done. Add more liquid as needed; the rice shouldn't be sticky.

Just before serving, sprinkle lots of freshly chopped cilantro over the top.

Serve with Quesadillas de Camarones (page 156), Barbecue Chicken and Pineapple Quesadillas (page 154), White Chicken Enchiladas (page 186), Fried Chicken Tacos (page 162), or Tequila Lime Chicken (page 170).

SUMMER STIR-FRY

Makes 8 to 10 servings

I love this fresh, light—and very, very quick and easy—skillet meal. Use whatever veggies you have, then chop, dice, or slice to your heart's content. All the beauty and deliciousness of late summer!

2 tablespoons butter

2 tablespoons olive oil

2 pounds jumbo shrimp, peeled and deveined, tails on

4 garlic cloves, minced

2 large zucchini, diced

2 ears of corn, kernels removed

¾ cup red grape tomatoes, sliced in half lengthwise

¾ cup yellow grape tomatoes, sliced in half lengthwise

Salt and freshly ground black pepper to taste

12 to 18 fresh basil leaves, cut in chiffonade

Juice of 1 lemon

Rice or pasta, for serving (optional)

1. Melt 1 tablespoon butter with 1 tablespoon olive oil in a large skillet over medium-high heat.

3. Remove the shrimp to a plate.

5. Stir it around for about 45 seconds . . .

2. Add the shrimp and garlic, then sauté until the shrimp are opaque, about 3 minutes.

4. Increase the heat to high, add the remaining 1 tablespoon butter and 1 tablespoon olive oil, and throw in the zucchini.

6. Then scoot the zucchini to the edges of the pan.

7. Throw in the corn and cook it for a minute . . .

8. Then push it to the edge of the pan.

9. Throw in the grape tomatoes . . .

10. Stir them around for a minute, then sprinkle on some salt . . .

11. And pepper.

12. Then throw the shrimp back in!

13. Stir everything around for about 45 seconds, or until it's all combined and hot.

14. Then pour it onto a big platter.

15. Sprinkle on the fresh basil, then—this is the best part— squeeze the lemon all over the top. This adds a wonderful, indescribable freshness.

You can serve this with rice . . . or with pasta. But it's just perfect on its own!

Variations

- Use any variety of vegetables: sliced mushrooms, diced carrots, and so on.

- Add a good splash of heavy cream to the skillet during the final minute of cooking for some added richness.

- Place some of the mixture in between two corn tortillas with some grated cheese. Cook on a griddle: veggie quesadilla!

PEACH-WHISKEY CHICKEN

Makes 6 to 8 servings

This is a fabulous throw-together meal that's as perfect on a Wednesday night with your family as it is on a Saturday night with friends. The results are impressive, as if you've slaved over a hot stove for hours.

I love that quality in a recipe.

2 tablespoons olive oil

2 tablespoons butter

12 chicken legs, skin-on

1 yellow onion, diced

1½ cups whiskey

4 cups barbecue sauce

1 cup peach preserves

2 tablespoons Worcestershire sauce

4 peaches, pitted and sliced into 8 slices each

Mashed potatoes, for serving

3 green onions, thinly sliced

Chopped fresh parsley

1. Preheat the oven to 300°F.

2. Heat the olive oil and butter in a large skillet or pot over medium-high heat. Cook the chicken pieces until golden brown on all sides, about 5 minutes.

3. Remove from the skillet and set aside.

4. Add the onion to the skillet.

5. Stir and cook over medium heat for about 3 minutes, or until translucent.

6. Pour in the whiskey, taking care if you're cooking over an open flame.

7. Cook for 3 minutes or so, allowing the whiskey to cook and reduce.

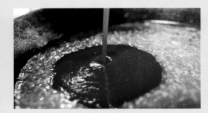

8. Grab your favorite bottled barbecue sauce . . .

9. And pour it into the pan.

10. Add the peach preserves, Worcestershire sauce, and ½ cup water to the sauce, then whisk to combine.

11. Add the chicken back to the pan . . .

12. Then throw in the peaches.

13. Cover the skillet with a lid or aluminum foil, then place in the oven for 1½ hours.

14. By then, the chicken is tender and falling off the bone . . . the sauce is beautiful and rich . . . and the peaches are soft. That's when you know it's done!

15. Serve the chicken over a big mound of mashed potatoes, spooning sauce over the whole thing. Sprinkle with the green onions and parsley, then watch your loved ones gobble it up.

Variations

- *Add several dashes of hot sauce for heat.*
- *Use whole chicken thighs instead of legs. (Divine.)*
- *Serve over buttered egg noodles.*
- *Substitute apricot preserves and sliced apricots.*

TANGY TOMATO BRISKET

Makes 8 servings

I love slow-cooked meat of any kind, and brisket is one of my very favorite cuts. This is actually known as "Passover Brisket" in some circles, and it's so darn simple and delicious, I'm always trying to figure out what the catch is. Serve it up with mashed potatoes and a green salad and your family will be eating out of your hand.

But only if your hand is holding this brisket.

One 5- to 8-pound beef brisket, trimmed of all fat (the butcher can do this for you)

One 24-ounce bottle ketchup or chili sauce

1 package dry onion soup mix

1. Preheat the oven to 275°F.

2. Place the brisket in an oven-safe pan.

3. Combine the ketchup and soup mix in a bowl . . .

4. Then stir it around to mix.

5. Pour in 1 cup water and stir to combine.

6. Pour the sauce all over the brisket, then flip the brisket over to coat the other side. Now just cover the pan with foil and roast in the oven for 6 to 7 hours.

7. Remove the pan from the oven and test the brisket to make sure it's fork-tender. The brisket should fall apart if you look at it!

8. Slice the brisket into thin strips . . .

9. And continue until it's all sliced up.

10. Then return the beef to the sauce and keep it warm until you're ready to serve.

Variations

- *Add hot sauce to the ketchup mixture for a spicier brisket.*

- *Serve with Fancy Mac and Cheese (page 132), Twice-Baked New Potatoes (page 212) and Panfried Kale (page 214), or Perfect Potatoes au Gratin (page 226).*

Note: This is a great thing to deliver to a new mama. The rich flavor really hits the spot.

Every day is a gravel road . . .

APRICOT SHRIMP SKEWERS

Makes 6 to 8 servings

These simple, delicious shrimp skewers can be adorned with any stone fruit you have around: apricots, peaches, nectarines. Red onion chunks give the skewers a nice crunch, and a sweet roasted jalapeño glaze gives them the perfect kick.

Make these in abundance—they disappear quickly!

4 fresh jalapeños

½ cup apricot preserves

4 apricots, pitted

1 red onion, halved and peeled

1 pound large shrimp, peeled and deveined

Chopped fresh cilantro to taste

1. Begin by soaking bamboo skewers in water for at least an hour. This keeps the skewers from going up in smoke when you're grilling.

2. Begin by roasting the jalapeños over an open burner or grill. (Alternatively, you can blacken them under the broiler in your oven.)

3. Keep them on the fire until the skin is totally black . . .

4. Then pop them into a plastic storage bag and seal them inside.

5. While the jalapeños are steaming, pour the preserves into a bowl.

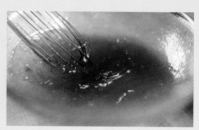

6. Add ½ cup water and whisk it together to thin.

7. Remove the jalapeños from the bag and use a knife to scrape off the blackened skin.

8. Chop the roasted jalapeños, discarding most of the seeds and inner membranes. Stir the chopped jalapeños into the glaze. Set the glaze aside while you assemble the skewers.

12. Then rinse the shrimp under cool water. We're ready to build the skewers!

15. Grill the skewers over medium heat. Divide the glaze in half in 2 separate bowls.

9. Slice the apricots into 6 wedges . . .

13. Thread the shrimp through the tail and top to keep it in place.

16. Turn them over, then brush on the jalapeño glaze from one of the bowls. Continue grilling until the shrimp are opaque and the apricots have nice grill marks.

10. Then cut the wedges in half to create chunks.

17. Remove them to a clean plate. Use the fresh unused batch of glaze (and a clean brush) to brush on more glaze at the end.

14. Then build the skewers to your heart's content. Be sure to double up the apricot chunks so they really make their mark on society.

11. Cut the red onion into chunks.

18. Sprinkle on cilantro and serve immediately. Serve with rice or pasta.

Variations

• *Add chunks of red, yellow, and green bell peppers to the skewers.*

• *Substitute pineapple chunks for the apricot chunks.*

• *Substitute jalapeño jelly for the apricot jelly for more spice and omit the roasted jalapeños.*

WHITE CHICKEN ENCHILADAS

Makes 8 servings

Yum. Seriously. This dish is everything that's wonderful about enchiladas, but with a chicken/cream approach. I roasted a bunch of bell and chile peppers—whatever I could find in my fridge—to give the sauce a nice color and flavor. Invite some buddies over for this one; it's a crowd-pleaser!

1 green bell pepper

1 red bell pepper

1 yellow bell pepper

2 or 3 hot chiles, such as jalapeños, serranos, or the like

1 large onion, diced

1 jalapeño, seeded and finely diced

1 tablespoon canola oil

2½ cups shredded cooked chicken

3 cups low-sodium chicken broth, plus more as needed

1½ cups heavy cream

1 teaspoon paprika

Dash of salt

4 tablespoons (½ stick) butter

¼ cup all-purpose flour

2½ cups grated Monterey Jack cheese

1 cup sour cream, plus more for serving

16 small corn tortillas

Cilantro, for serving

Salsa (page 92), for serving

1. Preheat the oven to 350°F.

2. Begin by roasting the bell peppers and chiles on a grill (or directly under the broiler) until the skin is mostly black.

3. Throw the chiles into a plastic storage bag and seal it. Let them steam inside the bag for 30 minutes or so.

5. Chop them up, then set them aside for a bit.

4. Core and seed the peppers, then scrape off the black skin.

6. In a large skillet over medium heat, sauté the onion and jalapeño in the canola oil until the onion is translucent, 2 to 3 minutes.

7. Throw in the chicken . . .

8. Then stir in 1 cup of the chicken broth . . .

9. And 1 cup of heavy cream.

10. Add ½ teaspoon of the paprika and the salt . . .

11. Then add half of the chopped peppers. Stir the mixture around and let it cook for a couple of minutes, then set it aside.

12. In a separate skillet over medium-high heat, melt the butter.

13. Sprinkle in the flour . . .

14. And whisk it together to combine. Cook, whisking constantly, for 1 minute.

15. Then pour in the remaining 2 cups of chicken broth, stirring constantly.

16. Stir and cook until the mixture is smooth, 1 to 2 minutes.

17. Then pour in the remaining ½ cup heavy cream . . .

18. The remaining ½ teaspoon paprika, and 1½ cups of the grated cheese.

19. Finally, stir in the sour cream and the rest of the chopped peppers. If the sauce needs a little thinning, splash in as much broth as you need. Give the sauce a taste and add salt if it needs it (with all the cheese, it shouldn't need much).

20. Warm the tortillas in the microwave until they're very soft.

21. Place a small amount of the chicken mixture and a small amount of cheese in the center of a tortilla.

22. Fold over the edges . . .

23. Then place them seam side down in a baking pan.

24. Pour the sauce over the top. My goodness.

25. Sprinkle the top with the remaining 1 cup grated cheese and bake for 20 to 25 minutes, or until bubbly.

26. Serve with a dollop of sour cream, a sprig of cilantro on top, and a small dish of salsa on the side.

These enchiladas will make your skirt fly up in a major way. Translation: They're delicious!

Variations

- *Substitute shrimp or shredded pork for the chicken.*

- *Serve with Mexican Rice (page 173) and/or refried black beans.*

- *Serve with Watermelon Granita (page 120) or Mango Margaritas (page 116).*

HERB-ROASTED PORK TENDERLOIN

Makes 8 to 10 servings

Pork . . . parsnips . . . preserves . . . and polenta (also known as cornmeal). You'll love this elegant meal.

ROASTED VEGETABLES

1 whole celery root, peeled and diced

3 whole parsnips, peeled and diced

6 whole carrots (varied colors if you can find them), peeled and diced

Other vegetables, peeled and diced (turnips, butternut squash, etc.)

Olive oil, for drizzling

Salt and black pepper to taste

CORNMEAL CAKES

2 cups cornmeal

6 cups chicken broth

Salt to taste

Olive oil, for frying

PORK

2 pork tenderloins, 1 to 1½ pounds each

Salt and black pepper to taste

½ cup herbes de Provence (sold in the spice aisle)

1 cup fig, peach, or plum preserves

1 tablespoon vinegar

1. Preheat the oven to 425°F.

2. To make the roasted vegetables, peel the vegetables.

3. Cut them into a uniform dice . . .

4. Then toss with olive oil, salt, and pepper.

5. Roast them in the oven for 15 to 20 minutes, or until the veggies are golden brown and starting to caramelize. Remove them from the oven and set aside.

6. Meanwhile, make the cornmeal cakes. Add the cornmeal to a pot with the chicken broth and salt.

7. Bring to a boil, then cover and simmer until the cornmeal is done, about 25 minutes.

8. Pour it onto a baking sheet.

9. Then spread it out into an even layer and allow it to cool to room temperature.

10. When the cornmeal mixture has cooled, cut a square, then cut the square in half diagonally.

11. Fry the cakes in olive oil in a skillet over medium-high heat.

12. Remove them when they're golden brown and drain them on a paper towel. Set aside.

13. Lay the pork tenderloins on a sheet pan and sprinkle them with salt and pepper.

14. Sprinkle on the herbes de Provence, then roast in the oven for 13 to 15 minutes, or until no longer pink in the middle. (Pork will continue to cook slightly after you remove it from the oven.)

15. Allow the pork to rest for 10 minutes, then slice it into thick pieces.

16. Meanwhile, stir together the preserves, the vinegar, and 1 cup water in a small pan or skillet. Heat over medium heat until thoroughly warmed, then set aside.

Hay Monsters are the bomb. They make hauling hay fun! Well . . . relatively speaking.

The minute our babies are weaned, we hand 'em a pair of work gloves.

Okay, the SECOND our babies are weaned.

17. Arrange 3 slices of pork over 2 cornmeal cakes.

18. Spoon the preserves over the top . . .

19. Then decorate the whole plate with the roasted vegetables. Beautiful and delicious!

Variations

- Toss root vegetables with buttered egg noodles and serve instead of cornmeal cakes.
- Substitute Risotto (page 194) or Grits (page 200) for the cornmeal cakes.

OSSO BUCO

Makes 8 servings

If you don't love osso buco . . . then you've never tried osso buco. True osso buco is made with veal shanks, which have exposed bones with crazy-delicious (once it's been slow cooked forever) bone marrow inside. The whole osso buco experience is utterly divine. Perfect for a special occasion!

OSSO BUCO

8 veal shanks

Kosher salt and black pepper to taste

2 tablespoons butter

2 tablespoons olive oil

3 garlic cloves, peeled

Two 12-ounce bottles dark beer

One 28-ounce can whole tomatoes

1 rosemary sprig

1 thyme sprig

RISOTTO

16 ounces baby portobello mushrooms, thickly sliced

½ cup olive oil

12 ounces baby spinach

1 onion, diced

2 cups arborio rice

4 cups chicken broth, heated

1 cup grated Parmesan cheese, plus more for serving

Crusty bread, for serving

1. Preheat the oven to 300°F.

2. Season the veal shanks with salt and pepper.

3. Heat the butter and oil in a heavy pot over high heat, then add the veal shanks.

4. Sear both sides of the veal until golden brown. Remove them from the pot and set aside.

5. Throw the garlic cloves into the pot . . .

6. And pour in the beer. Allow to bubble up and cook for about 5 minutes.

7. Return the veal shanks to the pot.

8. Crush the tomatoes with your hands . . .

9. Then pour them into the pot.

10. Throw in the rosemary and thyme.

11. Cover the pot and cook in the oven for 3 to 4 hours, or until the meat is fork-tender and the sauce is thick, rich, and gorgeous. Keep the lid on until you're ready to serve.

12. Meanwhile, make the risotto. Preheat the oven to 425°F. Drizzle the mushrooms with some olive oil.

13. Roast for 20 minutes, stirring once halfway through. The mushrooms will be a deep golden brown. (You may prepare the mushrooms ahead of time if oven space is an issue. Just keep them in the fridge until you need them.)

14. To wilt the spinach, heat a skillet over medium-high heat. Drizzle in some olive oil and cook the spinach for just 1½ to 2 minutes. Remove it from the heat and set aside.

15. In a heavy saucepan or pot, cook the onion in 1 tablespoon of olive oil over medium-high heat until soft, about 2 minutes.

16. Add the rice and cook, stirring, for 1 minute.

17. Add 1 cup of the warm broth, stirring and cooking until the broth is absorbed. Continue this process until all the broth is gone and the risotto is tender (it should still have a bite to it).

18. When the risotto is done, add the mushrooms and Parmesan and stir to combine.

19. To serve, heap the risotto on a plate. Top with the wilted spinach.

20. Add 1 or 2 veal shanks on top of the spinach (depending on appetite!) and spoon sauce on the top and around the sides.

Sprinkle with extra Parmesan and serve immediately. Crusty bread is a nice bonus.

Variations

- *Remove the veal from the sauce at the end and stir 1 cup heavy cream into the sauce for richness.*

- *Instead of risotto, serve Osso Buco with mashed potatoes or buttered noodles or (why not?) macaroni and cheese.*

- *Substitute beef short ribs for the veal shanks. Not technically Osso Buco, but still delicious and a little easier to come by!*

- *Serve with Buttered Rosemary Rolls (page 228).*

HONEY-PLUM-SOY CHICKEN

Makes 8 servings

When my good friend and fellow homeschooling mother Tiffany Poe made this, her signature dish, for me, my life as I knew it changed forever. It's a hearty chicken dish that's comforting (and simple) enough for a weeknight meal, but with a scrumptious Asian edge that can catapult it into dinner party cuisine fit for a king. Or a governor. Or a mayor. Or a county commissioner. Whatever fits your life.

8 bone-in, skin-on chicken thighs

3 cups red wine

3 bay leaves

One 13-ounce jar plum preserves

1 cup honey

One 20-ounce bottle soy sauce

2 tablespoons olive oil

4 garlic cloves, minced

**4 plums, pitted and chopped, plus
1 plum, pitted and thinly sliced**

12 ounces egg noodles

3 green onions, sliced

1. Put the chicken thighs in a large bowl. Pour in 2 cups of the red wine.

2. Add the bay leaves, toss to coat, and marinate for 1 hour in the fridge.

3. In a separate bowl, add the plum preserves . . .

4. Honey . . .

5. And soy sauce.

6. Whisk to combine and set aside.

7. Heat the olive oil in a heavy pot over medium-high heat. Remove the chicken from the wine, then brown on both sides, about 2 minutes per side.

8. Reduce the heat to medium-low, then add the garlic. Stir it around in the bottom of the pan for a couple of minutes to release the flavor.

9. Add the remaining cup of wine . . .

10. Chopped plums . . .

11. And honey-plum-soy mixture.

12. Bring to a boil, then reduce the heat to a simmer. Cover and simmer for 1½ to 2 hours, until the chicken is falling off the bone.

13. Cook the noodles according to the package directions and place on a large platter.

14. Spoon the chicken and at least half the cooking liquid over the noodles.

15. Serve the noodles and chicken on plates. Garnish with the plum slices and a sprinkling of sliced green onion, and have little bowls of extra cooking liquid on the table so people can spoon on more if desired. You will absolutely, positively go crazy over this. The flavors are out of this world.

Variations

- Add 2 teaspoons red pepper flakes to the cooking liquid for a spicier dish.

- Serve with Asian noodles instead of egg noodles.

- Use cherry preserves and pitted cherries instead of plums.

- This recipe works beautifully with duck breast for an even fancier-schmancier dish.

PORK CHOPS WITH APPLES AND GRITS

Makes 6 servings

I was tempted to call this dish "Pork Chops and Applesauce" as a nod to Peter Brady . . . but since the apples are still in chunks, I didn't want to confuse people.

I'm so glad we had this talk.

GRITS

8 slices bacon, cut into ½-inch pieces

1 yellow onion, chopped

2 cups stone-ground grits (the coarser, the better!)

4 cups low-sodium chicken broth

2 cups heavy cream (sorry . . .)

Dash of cayenne, or to taste

1½ cups grated Monterey Jack or other cheese

Salt and black pepper to taste

PORK

2 tablespoons butter

2 tablespoons olive oil

Six ½-inch-thick boneless pork chops

Dash of salt

Freshly ground black pepper

2 unpeeled Gala apples, cored and diced

½ cup dry white wine

2 teaspoons apple cider vinegar

¾ cup pure maple syrup

1. To make the grits, in a large pot over medium heat, cook the bacon and onion until the bacon is chewy and the onion is translucent, about 1 minute.

4. Stir together and bring to a boil, then reduce to a simmer, cover, and cook for 30 to 40 minutes, stirring occasionally.

2. Pour in the grits . . .

5. Add the cream and cayenne . . .

3. And the chicken broth.

6. And stir it into the grits.

7. Keep cooking over very low heat, covered, for another 20 to 30 minutes, or until the grits are tender but still have a bite to them. Stir them occasionally to keep them from sticking.

9. To make the pork chops, melt the butter with the oil in a large skillet over medium-high heat.

11. Then cook them in the skillet until golden brown, about 2 minutes per side. (They'll finish cooking in the pan later.)

8. Just before serving, stir in the cheese. Add salt and pepper to taste.

10. Season the pork chops on both sides with salt and pepper . . .

12. Remove the pork chops to a plate, then add the apples.

Sittin' on the dock of the pond.

13. Pour in the wine . . .

14. And the vinegar.

15. Cook the apples for 5 minutes, or until the liquid reduces by half.

16. Pour in the maple syrup.

17. Stir it in and allow it to come to a bubble.

18. Add the pork chops to the pan, then reduce the heat to low, cover the pan, and cook for another 20 minutes.

19. To serve, spoon a generous helping of grits onto a plate.

20. Lay a pork chop on top of the grits, then spoon the apples over the top. Be sure to get a little extra pan sauce onto the plate.

This is absolutely, positively delicious, guys. You'll love everything about it!

Variations

- *Add 1 teaspoon herbs de Provence to the apple mixture while it cooks.*

- *Serve with Panfried Kale (page 214) or Panfried Spinach (page 216).*

- *Substitute (slightly flattened) chicken breasts for the pork chops.*

A feed truck is a cow's best friend. At least from November to February.

RIB-EYE STEAK WITH ONION–BLUE CHEESE SAUCE

Makes 4 servings

There's something about blue cheese and beef. They're perfect companions, and if you think you don't like blue cheese . . . try this sauce. Just once. I beg you.

**4 rib-eye steaks
(about 5 ounces each)**

Salt and black pepper to taste

**8 tablespoons (1 stick) butter,
softened**

1 large yellow onion, sliced

1 cup heavy cream

**3 to 4 teaspoons
Worcestershire sauce**

¾ cup crumbled blue cheese

1. Preheat the grill to high heat.

2. Season the steaks with salt and pepper . . .

3. And smear both sides of the steaks with ½ stick (4 tablespoons) of the butter.

4. Grill the steaks until medium rare, 3 to 4 minutes per side, then remove from the heat and keep warm. (You can also sauté them in a skillet over medium-high heat if you prefer.)

5. Melt the remaining ½ stick butter in a large skillet over medium-high heat . . .

6. Then sauté the onion until golden brown, 7 to 8 minutes.

7. Pour in the cream . . .

8. Then add a dash of salt and pepper . . .

9. And the Worcestershire sauce.

10. Let it bubble up, then add the blue cheese . . .

11. And stir it together to melt the cheese, adding more pepper or Worcestershire as you wish.

12. Place the steaks on plates, then spoon the sauce over the top.

13. Take a bite. And the world, at long last, will make perfect sense.

Variations

- Include 8 ounces sliced mushrooms with the sautéed onions.

- Substitute sirloin or filet for the rib-eye.

- Serve with Twice-Baked New Potatoes (page 212), Panfried Kale (page 214), Panfried Spinach (page 216), Corn Casserole with Peppers (page 222), or Spicy Caesar Salad (page 40).

SPICY LEMON GARLIC SHRIMP

Makes 6 to 8 servings

While I'd be perfectly content to chow down on these delicious shrimp all by my lonesome, the fun, festive nature of the dish really lends itself well to a tableful of good buddies or extended family. Just lay down newspapers on the table, give everyone their own hunk of crusty, hot bread, and dive in!

Oh, and play John Denver in the background. "Poems, Prayers, and Promises," to be specific. Thank you for your cooperation.

1 cup (2 sticks) cold unsalted butter, cut into pieces

4 garlic cloves, peeled

¼ cup chopped fresh parsley

Juice of 2 lemons

1 teaspoon kosher salt

1 teaspoon crushed red pepper flakes

2 pounds raw shrimp, deveined, shells on

Crusty French bread, for serving

1. Preheat the oven to 375°F.

2. Add the butter and garlic to a food processer.

3. Then throw in the parsley . . .

4. Lemon juice . . .

5. Salt . . .

6. And red pepper flakes.

7. Pulse the mixture several times until everything is pulverized and mixed together.

8. Arrange the shrimp in a single layer on a large baking sheet.

9. Dot the top of the shrimp with the butter mixture, then put into the oven.

10. Roast the shrimp until they're cooked through and the butter is bubbly, about 20 minutes. Serve in a large bowl, making sure to drizzle all the juice over the top.

11. Encourage your guests to dip the bread into the juice at the bottom of the bowl as you sing along to the John Denver songs. That's the very best part.

Variation

Add 2 to 3 tablespoons of hot sauce to the butter mixture.

RANCH-STYLE CHICKEN

Makes 8 to 12 servings

This is based on one of my husband's favorite sandwiches; I just left the whole "sandwich" part out of it! Bacony, cheesy perfection on a plate.

6 whole boneless, skinless chicken breasts

½ cup honey

½ cup Dijon mustard

Juice of 1 lemon

1 teaspoon paprika

½ teaspoon salt

Crushed red pepper flakes to taste

1 pound thick-cut bacon, sliced in half and fried until chewy

3 tablespoons reserved bacon grease

2 cups grated sharp Cheddar cheese, or to taste

1. With a very sharp knife, cut the chicken breasts in half down the middle. This will result in 2 chicken breast pieces that are thinner and more uniform in size.

2. In a large bowl, combine the honey, Dijon . . .

3. Lemon juice . . .

4. Paprika . . .

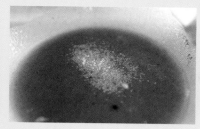

5. Salt, and crushed red pepper flakes. Stir to combine.

6. Add the chicken to the marinade and toss to coat. Cover the bowl with plastic wrap and marinate in the fridge for 2 to 4 hours.

7. When you're ready to cook the chicken, remove it from the marinade and grill it over medium-high heat, 3 to 4 minutes per side. Brush a little bacon grease on the chicken before placing it on the grill. (Or you can sauté them in a skillet over medium-high heat if you prefer.)

8. When a couple of minutes of grilling time are left, lay 2 pieces of bacon onto each chicken breast.

9. Top with some grated Cheddar and allow it to melt on the grill. (If you need to remove the chicken, you can finish melting the cheese under the broiler.)

Variations

- Serve with *Twice-Baked New Potatoes (page 212)* and a green salad.

- Slap it inside a bun and serve it to loved ones on the go.

SIDES

TWICE-BAKED NEW POTATOES

Makes 8 servings

These are a yummy, diminutive version of good ol' twice-baked potatoes, and maybe a tiny bit fancier.
But only a tiny bit.

12 new potatoes, scrubbed clean

2 tablespoons olive oil

4 ounces cream cheese, softened

½ cup sour cream

1½ cups grated Monterey Jack cheese

1 tablespoon minced chives

1 garlic clove, finely minced

Salt and black pepper to taste

"Hold me?"

1. Preheat the oven to 375°F.

2. Drizzle the potatoes with the olive oil and toss them to coat.

3. Roast the potatoes for 20 to 25 minutes, or until they are tender and the skin is slightly crisp.

4. Halve the potatoes. Use a spoon or small scoop to remove the insides, leaving a small margin of potato intact.

5. To the scooped-out potatoes, add the cream cheese, sour cream . . .

6. Monterey Jack, chives, garlic, and salt and pepper to taste.

7. Mash until the potato mixture is totally smooth. Give it a taste and add more salt if needed.

8. Scoop the mixture into the potato shells. At this point, you can cover and refrigerate them until dinnertime.

9. Bake the potatoes for 20 to 25 minutes, or until golden brown on top. Serve with steaks, chicken, or just a nice green salad and a glass of wine.

Enjoy!

Variation

Add a little goat cheese to the potato mixture for extra creaminess.

Hint: You can make these up to 3 days ahead of time and store, unbaked, in the fridge.

PANFRIED KALE

Makes 6 to 8 servings

I don't know where along the way kale got placed on the back burner of delicious veggies, but when I tasted a plateful of panfried kale well into adulthood, I felt like I'd been cheated my whole life. Beautiful texture, beautiful color, beautiful taste. You'll make it a permanent part of your side dish rotation, and you'll feel more and more like a health nut with each bite. It's so, so good for you.

1 large bunch kale, any variety
3 tablespoons olive oil

5 or 6 garlic cloves, finely minced

Salt and black pepper to taste

1. Thoroughly rinse the kale in cold water, soaking it in the water if it seems gritty or sandy. Tear the kale into chunks.

2. Heat the olive oil in a large skillet over medium-high heat. Add the garlic and quickly stir it around to avoid burning.

3. Throw in the kale . . .

4. And use tongs to move it around the skillet.

5. Sprinkle in plenty of salt and pepper . . .

6. And continue cooking until slightly wilted but still a little crisp, about 2 minutes.

7. Remove the kale to a plate and serve it to anyone who has a hankering for a huge dose of beta carotene and vitamin K!

This is one of my favorite healthy treats on earth.

PANFRIED SPINACH

Makes 2 to 4 servings

If Popeye's favorite veggie is more your cup of tea, substitute it for the kale. Just use the method on page 214!

1. Lotsa olive oil. Lotsa garlic. Lotsa heat.

2. Lotsa spinach . . . and just cook it for about 45 seconds!

3. Mmmm. Kale or spinach? How's a girl to decide?

CRASH HOT POTATOES

Makes 6 servings

Man, do I love Australia. First, my oldest daughter was conceived there on our honeymoon . . . and while we're on the subject, have I ever shared with you that we almost named her Sydney as a nod to her . . . um . . . point of origin? In the end, I chickened out, though—I thought that might be a little corny. Or awkward to explain. Or . . . never mind.

I also love Australia because of food writer Jill Dupliex, who first introduced me to these delicious smashed taters years and years ago. (Thank you, Jill, for changing my life with these little treats.)

I also love Australia because of Russell Crowe. But that's another story for another time.

12 whole new potatoes (or other small round potatoes)

Kosher salt to taste

3 tablespoons olive oil

Black pepper to taste

Minced rosemary (or other herb of choice) to taste

1. In a medium saucepan over medium heat, boil the potatoes in lightly salted water until fork-tender, about 20 minutes.

2. Preheat the oven to 450°F.

3. Place the potatoes on a baking sheet. Using a potato masher, gently press down to mash each one. Rotate the masher 90 degrees, then mash again.

4. Drizzle the tops of the potatoes with the olive oil.

5. Sprinkle generously with salt, pepper, and rosemary.

6. Bake for 20 to 25 minutes, or until golden brown and crisp. These are absolutely irresistible!

Variations

- *Place ¼ pat of butter on top of each smashed potato before baking.*

- *Top each smashed potato with grated Cheddar before baking.*

- *Serve with Rib-Eye Steak with Onion–Blue Cheese Sauce (page 204).*

GREEN BEAN CASSEROLE

Makes 8 servings

Green bean casserole from scratch? Yes, and it's a miracle. This is not your grandmother's green bean casserole.

Not that there's anything wrong with your grandmother's green bean casserole.

2 pounds fresh green beans, ends cut off

4 slices bacon, cut into ¼-inch pieces

½ large onion, chopped

3 garlic cloves, minced

4 tablespoons (½ stick) butter

4 tablespoons all-purpose flour

2½ cups whole milk

½ cup half-and-half

1½ teaspoons salt, plus more to taste

Freshly ground black pepper to taste

⅛ teaspoon cayenne pepper

1 cup grated sharp Cheddar cheese

One 4-ounce jar sliced pimentos, drained

Extra milk or chicken broth, for thinning if necessary

1 cup panko bread crumbs

1. Preheat the oven to 350°F.

2. Cut the green beans in half or thirds, depending on how bite-size you'd like them to be.

3. Blanch the green beans: drop them into lightly salted boiling water and cook for 3 to 4 minutes, until they're cooked through but still maintain a bit of snap.

4. Remove them from the boiling water with a slotted spoon and immediately plunge them into a bowl of ice cold water to stop the cooking process. Drain the cooled beans and set aside.

5. Add the bacon pieces to a skillet over medium heat. Cook the bacon for 2 minutes, then add the onion and garlic . . .

6. And continue cooking for 3 to 5 minutes, or until the bacon is cooked (but not crisp) and the onion is golden brown. Remove from the heat and set aside.

7. In a separate skillet or saucepan, melt the butter over medium heat.

8. Sprinkle the flour into the pan and whisk immediately to mix it evenly into the butter. Cook for a minute or two . . .

9. Then pour in the milk and half-and-half. Continue cooking, whisking constantly, while the sauce thickens, about 2 minutes.

10. Add the salt, pepper, cayenne, and grated Cheddar. Stir while the cheese melts. Turn off the heat.

11. Add the pimentos . . .

12. And the bacon/onion mixture. Stir to combine.

13. Place the green beans in a baking dish and pour the mixture on top.

14. Stir gently to combine.

15. Top with the panko bread crumbs.

16. Bake for 30 minutes, or until the sauce is bubbly and the panko bread crumbs are golden.

Take to a potluck dinner or serve on your holiday table. Yum!

Variations

• Add diced red bell pepper to the bacon/onion mixture before cooking instead of using jarred pimentos.

• Use Monterey Jack or Pepper Jack cheese for a lighter color.

ROASTED CAULIFLOWER

Makes 4 servings

Cauliflower is delicious raw, wonderful steamed . . . but miraculous roasted. Eat it straight out of the pan or top it with buttery bread crumbs and pop it back in the oven to crisp the top. A gorgeous side dish!

1 cauliflower head, cut into bite-size pieces

¼ cup olive oil

Salt and black pepper to taste

1½ cups panko bread crumbs

4 tablespoons (½ stick) butter, melted

1. Preheat the oven to 400°F.

2. Spread the cauliflower on a large sheet pan and drizzle it with the olive oil.

3. Toss the cauliflower to coat it evenly. Add salt and pepper to taste.

4. Roast the cauliflower for 15 to 20 minutes, or until golden brown with some darker parts.

5. Add the bread crumbs to a bowl . . .

6. Then pour in the melted butter and toss the bread crumbs to combine.

7. Place the cauliflower in a medium baking dish (or cute little individual dishes, as shown here), then mound the bread crumbs on top.

8. Roast for 5 minutes, or until the bread crumbs are golden brown on top. A perfect, yummy side dish.

Variations

- *Sprinkle with a little curry powder or some cumin seeds before roasting.*
- *Add minced fresh herbs to the bread crumbs.*
- *Add grated Cheddar or Parmesan to the bread crumbs!*

CORN CASSEROLE WITH PEPPERS

Makes 8 to 12 servings

Fresh corn cut off the cob and baked with butter and cream is about the best thing on earth. But if you add some diced bell peppers and jalapeños to the mix? *Fugghetaboutit.*

8 ears of corn, husked, kernels shaved off the cob

1 red bell pepper, seeded and diced

2 fresh jalapeños, seeded and diced (include some seeds if you'd like more heat)

½ cup (1 stick) butter

1 cup heavy cream

½ cup whole milk

Salt and black pepper to taste

1. Preheat the oven to 375°F.

2. Combine the corn, bell pepper, and jalapeños in a bowl.

3. Add the butter . . .

4. Cream, milk . . .

5. And salt and pepper to taste.

6. Pour into a buttered baking dish and bake for 20 to 25 minutes, or until hot and bubbly.

7. Give it a stir before serving in order to coat all the corn in the delicious cream/butter mixture under the surface.

Crunchy, crispy, creamy corn goodness!

Serve with steak, chicken, or shrimp.

WHISKEY-GLAZED CARROTS

Makes 6 to 8 servings

I used to make these only for holiday meals . . . but I loved them so much, I wound up turning them into a year-round side dish.

What can I say? The whiskey made me do it.

1 stick butter

2 pounds carrots, peeled and cut into ½-inch pieces

¾ cup Jack Daniel's or other whiskey

¾ cup packed brown sugar

Salt and freshly ground black pepper to taste

1 thyme sprig

1. Melt ½ stick of butter in a large skillet (with a lid) over high heat. Add half the carrots . . .

5. Reduce the heat to medium-low, add the other half stick of butter . . .

9. Reduce the heat to low, place the lid on the skillet, and cook for 5 minutes.

2. And stir them around to brown them quickly, about 1 minute.

6. And stir it around until it's melted.

10. Remove the lid and cook for another 5 minutes. Sprinkle in salt and pepper to taste. Be sure to add enough salt to offset the sweetness!

3. Remove them to a clean plate and repeat with the remaining carrots.

7. Stir in the brown sugar . . .

4. Pour the whiskey into the skillet, taking care if you're cooking over an open flame. Let the whiskey bubble up and cook for 3 minutes, or until slightly reduced.

8. Then add the carrots.

11. Serve with a thyme sprig or sprinkle chopped thyme on the top.

The color will draw you in . . . the butter and whiskey will make you stay.

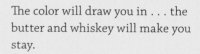

PERFECT POTATOES AU GRATIN

Makes 8 servings

There's potatoes au gratin . . . and then there's *potatoes au gratin*. This is the second kind, and it will rock your ever-loving world. Serve them with steak, chicken, burgers; I promise you they'll steal the show.

2 tablespoons butter, softened

4 large russet potatoes, scrubbed clean

½ cup whole milk

1½ cups heavy cream

2 tablespoons all-purpose flour

3 garlic cloves, finely minced

1 teaspoon salt

Freshly ground pepper to taste

1 cup freshly grated sharp Cheddar cheese

2 green onions, thinly sliced (white and light green parts only)

1. Preheat the oven to 400°F. Butter a baking dish with the softened butter.

2. Begin by slicing the potatoes into sticks.

3. Then slice up the sticks to create a dice.

4. Combine the milk and cream in a bowl.

5. Add the flour . . .

6. Minced garlic . . .

7. And plenty of salt and pepper.

8. Whisk it together well so that the flour is incorporated into the milk/cream mixture.

9. Add the diced potatoes to a large baking dish and pour the creamy mixture all over the top.

10. Cover the dish with foil and bake it for 30 minutes. Remove the foil and bake for 20 minutes more. Just before serving, sprinkle on the grated cheese and return it to the oven for 3 to 5 minutes, or until the cheese is melted and bubbly.

11. Sprinkle on the green onions and serve it hot.

Variations

- Use thinly sliced potatoes instead of diced: scalloped potatoes!

- Use whatever cheese(s) you'd like: Monterey Jack, goat cheese, farmer's cheese, Swiss, and so on.

- Add diced ham to make this a main course.

BUTTERED ROSEMARY ROLLS

Makes however many rolls you'd like!

These are the easiest, most delicious dinner rolls, warm and soft, with the most delectable rosemary flavor. They go with so many main dishes—beef, chicken, seafood, even pasta—and they disappear very, very quickly.

Butter

Frozen unbaked, unrisen dinner rolls

Coarsely chopped fresh rosemary to taste

Coarse sea salt to taste

1. Melt 1 tablespoon butter in an iron skillet over medium-low heat. Remove from the heat and cool for 10 minutes.

2. Place the dinner rolls in the warm skillet, allowing some space between the rolls.

3. Cover with a dish towel or cloth napkin and set aside in a warm place to rise for at least 2 hours.

4. When risen, the rolls will be poufy and soft.

5. Melt 2 tablespoons butter, then brush the butter onto the rolls.

6. Then sprinkle the rolls with chopped rosemary.

7. Finally, sprinkle with sea salt.

8. Bake for 15 to 20 minutes at 350°F. Don't be alarmed if you pull them out of the oven and they've risen way over the surface of the pan. Within a minute or two, they'll calm right down.

Then you can dig right in!

"From now on, I'd like you to call me Swishie."

SWEETS

DULCE DE LECHE COFFEE

Makes 6 servings

I whipped this up one bitterly cold afternoon a couple of years ago when we couldn't leave our house because of the snowdrifts. I don't always add the booze . . . but it's extra good when I do.

4 cups good, hot, strongly brewed coffee

6 ounces dulce de leche (see Note)

2 tablespoons sugar

1 cup heavy cream

6 tablespoons Kahlúa, more if preferred

Small chunk of dark chocolate

Cocoa nibs or chopped semisweet chocolate, for garnish (optional)

Note: Dulce de leche is sold in the Hispanic aisle of supermarkets or in Hispanic specialty markets. It is sold in solid blocks or in cans or jars.

1. Add the coffee to a pitcher or carafe.

2. Cut the dulce de leche into chunks (if you're using the solid variety) . . .

3. And drop them into the coffee. Let it sit and dissolve for 5 minutes. (If you're using liquid dulce de leche, just pour it into the coffee and stir to dissolve.)

4. Meanwhile, in a mixer bowl, add the sugar to the heavy cream . . .

5. And beat it until slightly stiff.

6. Pour the Kahlúa into serving glasses if using.

7. Stir the coffee to make sure the dulce de leche is dissolved, then divide it among the glasses.

8. Mmmm. This is good enough as it is.

9. But it's extra good if you pile on the whipped cream!

10. Zest or grate a little chocolate . . .

11. And sprinkle it on the top of each glass.

12. Finally, sprinkle on some cocoa nibs or chopped semisweet chocolate. This is one of the best cold-weather drinks there is.

APPLE DUMPLINGS

Makes 8 servings (2 dumplings per serving)

This dessert came from my mom's friend Donna, and when I made it for the first time, I did so on a lark. The ingredients were so out there . . . so crazy . . . I thought it had to be a joke.

When I took my first bite, I couldn't believe what I was experiencing. Some magical metamorphosis had occurred when the refrigerated crescent roll dough combined with the butter and the pop . . . it all turned into something that tasted like it came from a French bakery.

I can hear you laughing. Stop that! Just try it. Just once. You'll see what I mean.

Oh, and one more thing: Do you say pop? Or soda? Or Coke? Inquiring minds want to know.

2 Granny Smith apples

Two 8-ounce cans crescent roll dough

1 cup (2 sticks) butter

1½ cups sugar

1½ teaspoons vanilla extract

One 12-ounce can Mountain Dew

Ground cinnamon to taste

Vanilla or cinnamon ice cream, for serving

"No, I'm not cranky. Why do you ask?"

1. Preheat the oven to 350°F.

2. Peel the apples.

3. Core them and cut into 8 equal wedges.

4. Wrap each apple wedge in 1 piece of crescent roll dough, beginning at the wide end and ending at the point. Place the rolls seam side down in a buttered 8 x 10-inch baking dish.

5. Melt the butter in a medium saucepan over low heat.

6. Add the sugar and vanilla and stir for a few seconds. No need to dissolve the sugar; you want the mixture to be grainy.

7. Pour the butter/sugar mixture evenly over the rolls.

8. Next—and this is the crazy/radical part—pour the can of Mountain Dew all over the top. It'll look really liquidy and weird . . . but don't worry. It'll all make sense in the end.

9. Finally, sprinkle the top with cinnamon.

10. Bake for 40 minutes, or until golden brown.

11. Serve the dumplings with vanilla or cinnamon ice cream, spooning on some of the syrup from the bottom of the pan.

You won't believe how good these are. No, really. You seriously won't believe it.

Variations

- *Substitute ripe peach, pear, or apricot slices.*

- *Substitute ginger ale or lemon-lime soda for Mountain Dew.*

CITRUS BUTTER COOKIES

Makes approximately 24 cookies

I set out to make lemon butter cookies one day, but my limes and oranges staged a protest. They didn't want to be ignored! The result was a gloriously delightful cookie with all sorts of citrus love going on. That they also happen to be really pretty is just the icing on the cake.

Er . . . cookie.

Er . . . never mind.

COOKIES

2 large eggs

4 sticks (1 pound) salted butter, softened

1½ cups sugar

3 tablespoons orange, lemon, and lime zest (1 tablespoon each)

4 cups all-purpose flour

2 tablespoons orange, lemon, and/or lime juice (2 tablespoons total)

ICING

3 cups powdered sugar

2 tablespoons whole milk

2 tablespoons combined orange, lemon, and lime zest

Juice of ½ lime

Juice of ½ lemon

Dash of salt

Extra zest, for decorating

1. Preheat the oven to 350°F.

2. Separate the eggs. Set aside one of the egg whites for the icing.

3. Using a hand or stand mixer, cream the butter and sugar until combined.

4. Add the egg yolks and mix until combined.

5. Add the 3 tablespoons of citrus zest.

6. Then add the flour and mix until just combined.

7. Next, add the 2 tablespoons of citrus juice (your choice) and mix the dough until it comes together.

8. Scoop out heaping teaspoons of dough, then roll them into balls between your hands. Place them on a cookie sheet . . .

9. And bake them for 12 to 13 minutes, or until they're not quite starting to turn brown. Remove them from the oven but keep them on the cookie sheet for 3 to 4 minutes. Use a spatula to move them to a cooling rack and cool them completely.

10. To make the icing, combine 1 egg white with the rest of the icing ingredients (except the extra zest for sprinkling). Whisk thoroughly until combined, adding either more powdered sugar or more juice until it reaches a pourable but still thick consistency.

11. Drizzle the icing across the cookies in several lines, then repeat in the other direction.

12. Sprinkle them with extra zest before the icing sets.

TRES LECHES CAKE

Makes one 9 x 13-inch cake

Tres Leches Cake is one of the things they serve in Heaven. I'm absolutely sure of it. A Latin American dessert, Tres Leches is a moist, spongy cake that's doused in three different milk products. You can add berries or other fruits to make things a little fancier, or you can just leave it plain and enjoy the simple beauty of it. This is a treat that many people haven't discovered yet, and every time I serve it to someone in that category, I love to hear them ask, "What IS this?" It's always a hit.

1 cup all-purpose flour

1½ teaspoons baking powder

¼ teaspoon salt

5 large eggs, separated

1 cup plus 3 tablespoons sugar

⅓ cup whole milk

1 teaspoon vanilla extract

One 14-ounce can sweetened condensed milk

One 12-ounce can evaporated milk

1 pint plus ¼ cup heavy cream

Maraschino cherries, for garnish

1. Preheat the oven to 350°F and grease and flour a 9 x 13-inch baking pan.

2. Combine the flour, baking powder, and salt in a large bowl. Set aside.

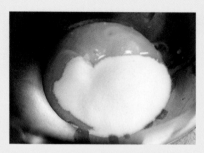

3. Add the egg yolks and ¾ cup of the sugar to a mixing bowl.

4. Beat them until very light in color . . .

5. Then add the milk and vanilla and beat until just combined.

6. Pour this over the flour mixture . . .

7. And stir gently to combine.

8. In a clean mixing bowl, beat the egg whites on high speed until soft peaks form. Add ¼ cup of the sugar, then continue beating until the whites are stiff but not dry.

9. Gently fold the egg whites into the bowl with the other ingredients. Don't overmix; stop just short of everything being totally mixed together.

10. Spread the batter in the baking pan and bake the cake for 35 to 45 minutes, or until a toothpick comes out clean.

11. Remove the cake from the oven and allow it to cool completely in the pan.

12. When the cake is cool, invert it onto a platter and poke holes in the surface with the tines of a fork.

13. Combine the sweetened condensed milk, evaporated milk, and ¼ cup heavy cream. I spy three milks!

14. Slowly douse the cake with the milk mixture, getting it all around the edges and evenly coating the surface. Much of the liquid will be absorbed into the cake, but expect some to pool here and there. This is normal.

And this is good.

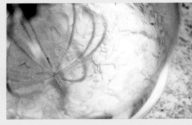

15. Allow the cake to sit and absorb the liquid for at least 30 minutes, then whip 1 pint heavy cream with the remaining 3 tablespoons of sugar until thick.

16. Spread it all over the top and sides of the cake.

17. Cut into squares and serve, decorating with a single cherry if you'd like. Keep leftovers refrigerated.

(Pssst: It's even more delicious the next day!)

Cowboy Consultation!

BILLIE'S ITALIAN CREAM CAKE

Makes one 9-inch round cake or 1 rectangular layer cake

Billie is a friend from church and once brought this classic layer cake to our house on the Fourth of July. It was the best Italian cream cake I'd ever tried, and when she saw how smitten I was, she shared the recipe with me.

That's what church friends are for.

CAKE

5 eggs, separated

½ cup (1 stick) butter

1 cup vegetable oil

1 cup granulated sugar

1 tablespoon vanilla extract

1 cup sweetened flaked coconut

2 cups all-purpose flour

1 teaspoon baking soda

1 teaspoon baking powder

1 cup buttermilk (or 1 cup milk mixed with 1 teaspoon white vinegar)

ICING

Two 8-ounce packages cream cheese

½ cup (1 stick) butter

2 teaspoons vanilla extract

2 pounds powdered sugar

1 cup chopped pecans

1 cup sweetened flaked coconut

1. Preheat the oven to 350°F. Grease and flour three 9-inch round cake pans or 2 quarter sheet pans or one 9 x 12-inch pan.

2. To make the cake, beat the egg whites until they're stiff. Transfer them to another bowl, then clean the mixing bowl and beater.

3. Combine the butter, vegetable oil, and granulated sugar in the mixing bowl and mix until light and fluffy. Add the egg yolks and vanilla, then beat until smooth.

4. Add the coconut and beat to combine.

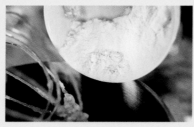

5. Combine the flour, baking soda, and baking powder in a medium bowl, then alternate adding the flour mixture . . .

6. And the buttermilk, mixing for a few seconds after each addition.

7. Add the egg whites and fold them in gently by hand until they're combined with the batter.

8. Pour the batter into the greased pans and spread it out. Bake the cakes for 15 to 18 minutes, or until a toothpick comes out clean.

9. Turn the cakes out of the pans and allow them to cool completely.

Redheads rule!

10. To make the icing, combine the cream cheese, butter, vanilla, and powdered sugar in a mixing bowl. Beat until very light and fluffy.

11. Chop up the pecans . . .

12. And add ¾ cup to the icing with the coconut.

13. Mix until it's all combined. Yum!

14. Stack the cake layers. (I baked them in 2 quarter sheet pans, then cut them in half lengthwise, winding up with 4 rectangular layers and spreading a generous amount of icing in between each layer.)

15. Spread extra icing all around the sides.

16. End with a sprinkling of the remaining chopped pecans.

(Psst: This is particularly delicious with coffee. Don't ask me how I know this.)

Store leftovers in the fridge.

Strike a pose.

POTS DE CRÈME

Makes 10 to 12 servings

Pots de crème are a cross between chocolate pudding and chocolate mousse and chocolate custard and . . . oh, never mind. They're chocolate. And they're creamy and dreamy and wonderful.

One important thing you need to know about *pots de crème* is how to pronounce it.

First of all, here's how you do *not* pronounce *pots de crème*: "pawts day creem."

Here's how you *do* pronounce *pots de crème*: "po duh krehm."

Or, if you want to get really technical, "po duh k(insert phlegmy, back-of-the-throat crackly French sound)ehm."

But you really don't need to pronounce it. You just need to eat it.

12 ounces semisweet chocolate chips

4 eggs, at room temperature

2 teaspoons vanilla extract

Pinch of salt

8 ounces very hot strong coffee

1 cup heavy cream

2 tablespoons sugar

1. Place the chocolate chips in the blender.

2. Crack in the eggs, then add the vanilla and salt.

3. Pulse 5 to 7 times, or until the chocolate chips are partially pulverized.

4. Turn on the blender, then pour in the very hot coffee in a steady stream. The coffee will melt the chocolate and turn it into a smooth mixture.

5. Pour the mixture into small mason jars, pretty wineglasses, or demitasse cups.

6. Place the jars on a tray and refrigerate them for 2 to 3 hours, or until firm.

7. Yum!

8. Whip the cream with the sugar, and plop it onto the top of each glass.

9. Such an easy, throw-together dessert, with such delicious results.

Me likey. And you will, too!

Variations

- *Add 2 to 3 tablespoons of whiskey or Grand Marnier to the blender with the chocolate chips and eggs.*

- *Add ¼ teaspoon mint extract for chocolate mint pots de crème.*

"Peace, Bro. I mean Ma."

STRAWBERRY SHORTCAKE CAKE

Makes one 10-inch cake

I made this cake a few years ago on a whim . . . and what a delightful whim it turned out to be. It's a spin on strawberry shortcake, but the cake is, well, cake—not the biscuit-like disc in the classic strawberry shortcake recipe. I added cream cheese frosting instead of whipped cream, just for kicks, and it turned out to be just what the whole mess of deliciousness needed.

This is one of my father-in-law's three favorite desserts. He likes to eat it for breakfast.

I do too, now that I think about it!

CAKE

½ cup (1 stick) plus 1 tablespoon unsalted butter, softened

1½ cups plus 3 tablespoons granulated sugar

3 large eggs

½ cup sour cream, at room temperature

1 teaspoon vanilla extract

1½ cups all-purpose flour

3 tablespoons cornstarch

½ teaspoon salt

1 teaspoon baking soda

STRAWBERRIES

1 pound strawberries, hulled and halved

3 tablespoons granulated sugar

CREAM CHEESE FROSTING

One 8-ounce package cream cheese, at room temperature

1 cup (2 sticks) unsalted butter

1½ pounds powdered sugar, sifted

1 teaspoon vanilla extract

¼ teaspoon salt

1. Preheat the oven to 350°. Grease and flour a 9-inch round cake pan *that's at least 2 inches deep* (or you can split the batter between 2 pans if they're not deep enough).

2. To make the cake batter, beat together the butter and sugar until fluffy. Add the eggs one at a time, beating well after each addition.

3. Add the sour cream and vanilla, then mix until just combined.

4. Sift together the flour, cornstarch, salt, and baking soda and add it to the bowl.

5. Mix it together until just combined.

6. Spread it in the pan or pans and bake for 45 to 50 minutes, or until the cake is no longer jiggly like my bottom.

9. Sprinkle the strawberries with the sugar. Toss them around and allow them to sit for a little while.

12. Mix until very light and fluffy. Warning: You'll feel like eating this bowl of icing before you even get it on the cake.

7. Carefully remove the cake from the pan and allow it to cool completely.

10. They'll give off this beautiful liquid after several minutes. Try not to drink it with a straw.

13. To assemble the cake, use a sharp knife to cut it in half through the middle. It's easier if you go all around the perimeter of the cake, slicing only halfway through the circle the whole way.

8. Next, mash the strawberries with a potato masher or a fork (reserve a few for garnish if you like).

11. To make the frosting, combine the cream cheese, butter, powdered sugar, vanilla, and salt in a mixing bowl.

14. Lay the two halves cut side up.

15. And cover both halves with an equal amount of strawberries. Then—this is an important step!—place the cake halves in the freezer for 15 to 20 minutes. This'll firm up the surface of the strawberries just a bit so that it's easier to spread on the icing.

18. Carefully ice the outside of the cake with the remaining icing.

19. Lovely! You can certainly decorate the top of the cake with strawberry slices, too.

But I'm hungry and want to eat, so I'll skip that part.

Store leftovers in the fridge. The cake can be made up to 24 hours in advance.

16. Remove the cakes from the freezer and place one layer on a cake stand or platter. Cover with a little less than a third of the icing.

17. Place the second layer on top, then spread the top with icing.

APPLE BROWN BETTY

Makes 8 to 10 servings

Apple Brown Betty is a very old, ridiculously easy throw-together dessert that must have been invented once upon a time in order to use up day-old bread. I love its simplicity, and I absolutely love how comforting and down-home it is. I've learned Apple Brown Betty is best if you use grainy wheat bread—but use whatever extra bread you might have lying around.

   Every time I make it, I can't help but feel like I'm living in a simpler time. Then I hear my cell phone ringing and I am violently thrust back into reality.

8 slices wheat bread

3 apples, preferably Granny Smith, peeled and cored

1½ cups packed brown sugar, more if needed

1 cup (2 sticks) salted butter

1 cup heavy cream

1 tablespoon granulated sugar

1. Preheat the oven to 375°F. Generously butter a 9 x 13-inch rectangular baking dish.

2. Slice the bread into strips . . .

3. Then slice the strips in the other direction to dice.

4. Cut the apples into slices . . .

5. Then dice them up, too.

6. Place half the diced bread in the baking dish . . .

7. Then sprinkle on half the diced apples . . .

8. And half the brown sugar.

9. Repeat with another layer of bread, apples, and brown sugar. Dot the top of the whole thing with pats of butter.

10. End by sprinkling ½ cup water all over the surface, a spoonful at a time.

11. Bake, covered in foil, for 45 minutes, or until the apples are tender. Remove the foil and bake for an additional 10 minutes to brown.

12. To serve, whip the heavy cream with the sugar until it's lightly beaten but still pourable. Dish up a generous portion of Apple Brown Betty onto a plate . . .

13. And drizzle on the cream.

Warm, sweet, comfort food. Life doesn't get much better than this.

Variations

- *Brown Betty can be made with peaches, pears, berries, or cherries.*
- *Use whole wheat bread, white bread . . . any bread will do!*

COFFEE CREAM CAKE

Makes one 2-layer 8- or 9-inch cake

I won't even attempt to describe it. All I can do is encourage you to make it as soon as possible. Today. *Right now.* It's beyond words. If you're a lover of coffee, it's twelve trips to Heaven and back.

CAKE

1 cup (2 sticks) butter

3 tablespoons instant coffee crystals

1 cup boiling water

2 cups all-purpose flour

2 cups granulated sugar

¼ teaspoon salt

½ cup buttermilk (or ½ cup milk mixed with ½ teaspoon white vinegar)

2 eggs

1 teaspoon baking soda

2 teaspoons vanilla extract

CREAMY FILLING

One 8-ounce package cream cheese, at room temperature

1 cup powdered sugar

1 cup heavy cream

COFFEE ICING

¾ cup (1½ sticks) butter

2 tablespoons instant coffee crystals

4 tablespoons half-and-half

4 cups powdered sugar

2 teaspoons vanilla extract

1. Preheat the oven to 350°F. Thoroughly grease and flour 2 round 8- or 9-inch baking pans.

2. To make the cake, melt the butter in a saucepan.

3. Sprinkle in the instant coffee . . .

4. And add the boiling water.

5. Let the mixture bubble up for a few seconds, then turn off the heat.

6. Add the flour, sugar, and salt to a large bowl. Pour the hot butter/coffee mixture over the top and stir to combine.

7. Mix together the buttermilk, eggs, baking soda, and vanilla, and pour it into the bowl.

8. Pour the batter evenly into the cake pans and bake for 13 to 15 minutes, or until set. Remove the pans from the oven and allow the cakes to cool inside the pans for 10 minutes, then invert the cake layers onto a work surface and allow to cool completely.

9. To make the creamy filling, add the cream cheese to a mixing bowl.

10. Add the powdered sugar . . .

11. And the heavy cream. Beat until light and fluffy, then set aside.

12. Next, make the coffee icing: Melt the butter in a saucepan and add the instant coffee.

13. Stir it together, then add the half-and-half and whisk together to combine.

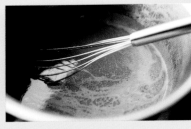

14. Turn off the heat.

15. Then add the powdered sugar and vanilla.

16. Whisk well to make the icing perfectly smooth, then let it cool for 5 minutes.

17. When the cake layers are completely cool, spread the creamy mixture on the bottom layer.

18. Transfer it to a cake stand, then gently lay the second layer on top.

19. Drizzle the coffee icing on top . . .

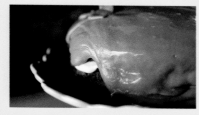

20. Allowing it to drip down the sides.

21. Swirl the icing around on the sides, then count how many seconds it takes you to cut a very enormous wedge and serve it to yourself.

22. That took me approximately 43 seconds. A new world record in patience, ladies and gents!

Variation

For a mocha cake, ice with your favorite chocolate icing/ganache instead.

"Where's my piece?"

BANANAS FOSTER

Makes 6 servings

Anyone who's known me for any length of time likely knows that I hate, abhor, loathe, and recoil at the sight of bananas. I've disliked them my entire life, even when I was a baby, and I'll dislike them till I croak.

That I'm including a recipe that contains bananas in my cookbook is a testament to how darn delicious it is.

Be very careful when cooking with alcohol and an open flame.

½ cup (1 stick) salted butter

1 cup packed dark brown sugar

½ cup heavy cream

2 bananas, sliced diagonally into thick slices

½ cup chopped walnuts or pecans

½ cup dark rum

Dash of cinnamon

Vanilla Bean Ice Cream (page 266), for serving

1. Melt the butter in a heavy skillet over medium-high heat.

2. Add the brown sugar.

3. Stir together and continue cooking for a minute or two.

4. Pour in the cream . . .

5. And stir it around to combine.

6. Peel the bananas and slice them on the bias inside the peel.
Bananas. BLECH!
(That was me recoiling at the sight of bananas.)

7. Then just drop them into the pan.

8. Next, add the chopped nuts and stir them into the sauce.

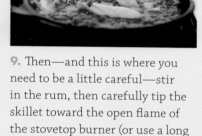

9. Then—and this is where you need to be a little careful—stir in the rum, then carefully tip the skillet toward the open flame of the stovetop burner (or use a long lighter to ignite it).

10. Let the fire burn and go out (it'll only take about 30 seconds or so) . . .

11. Then stir in the cinnamon at the end.

12. Spoon it over a couple of scoops of Vanilla Bean Ice Cream and enjoy it immediately.

If you aren't a banana fan, this might be the one exception to the rule! And even if you don't like the bananas themselves, you'll want to drink the sauce with a straw.

Variations

- *You may simply cook the mixture without flambéing it.*

- *Spoon Bananas Foster over French toast, waffles, or crepes.*

- *Substitute peaches, pears, or cherries for the bananas. Of course, then it probably wouldn't be considered Bananas Foster.*

Pond? Or Paradise? You decide.

KNOCK YOU NAKED BROWNIES

Makes one 9 x 9-inch pan of brownies

I was once gifted with a tin of brownies by a very kind soul. It was a tin of Killer Brownies from Dorothy Lane Market in Dayton, Ohio. And these weren't just any brownies: They were multilayered wonders with gorgeous caramel oozing out of the center layer. And the flavor: to die for! I ate them over a period of several days, more despondent with each bite that I was one step closer to being without them.

They were one of the best things I'd ever tasted.

While an official recipe for the Dorothy Lane Killer Brownie is not available, this classic old layered brownie recipe is rumored to be a very close match.

(For the record, I have no clue as to the origin of this recipe name. But that's probably just as well.)

⅓ cup plus ½ cup evaporated milk

One 18.5-ounce box German chocolate cake mix

½ cup (1 stick) butter, melted

1 cup finely chopped pecans

60 caramels, unwrapped

⅓ cup semisweet chocolate chips

¼ cup powdered sugar, sifted

1. Preheat the oven to 350°F. Grease and flour a 9 x 9-inch baking pan.

2. Begin by pouring ⅓ cup evaporated milk into a bowl with the cake mix.

3. Add the melted butter . . .

4. And the chopped pecans.

5. Mix the ingredients together. It'll be pretty thick!

6. Divide the dough in half down the middle . . .

7. And press it into the bottom of the pan to make the first brownie layer.

8. Bake for 8 to 10 minutes, or until set, then remove it from the oven and set aside.

9. While the brownie layer is baking, in a double boiler (or a glass bowl set over a bowl of simmering water), combine the caramels and ½ cup evaporated milk.

10. Stir occasionally until the caramels are totally melted and the mixture is smooth.

11. Pour the caramel mixture over the first baked layer, spreading it so that it's evenly distributed.

12. Sprinkle the chocolate chips all over the top.

13. Next, on a clean surface or a sheet of wax paper, press the remaining brownie dough into a square shape slightly smaller than the baking pan.

14. Carefully set it on top of the chocolate chips . . .

15. And bake it for 20 to 25 minutes. Remove the pan from the oven and let the brownies cool to room temperature. Cover the pan and refrigerate the brownies for several hours to allow them to set.

16. When you're ready to serve them (or package them up for a friend!), sprinkle them generously with the powdered sugar and cut them into large rectangles before removing them from the pan.

17. These are absolutely killer, my friends. Make them for someone you really, really love . . . or someone you want to love you back.

It'll work. I guarantee it.

Variation

Cut brownies into smaller squares, if desired, and shake in a plastic bag of powdered sugar. (Make sure they're cold and set first!)

Um! You said "naked"!

BLACKBERRY CHIP ICE CREAM

About 1½ pints

My friend Ryan from Cincinnati visited the ranch a few years ago, his fully tattooed arms and his beautiful family in tow. Along with a few cans of Skyline Chili (a Cincy favorite) Ryan also brought along a pint of Graeter's (another Cincy favorite) Black Raspberry Chip ice cream packed on dry ice. I'd never tasted a more delicious ice cream.

   Since I don't have a Graeter's anywhere near my little house on the prairie, I figured out how to whip up a similar version myself. Such a uniquely delicious treat.

2 pints fresh blackberries

1¼ cups sugar

Juice of ½ lemon

1½ cups half-and-half

5 egg yolks

1½ cups heavy cream

4 ounces semisweet chocolate

1. Combine the blackberries, ¼ cup of the sugar, and the lemon juice in a saucepan. Cook over low heat for about 20 minutes, or until the blackberries are broken down and syrupy.

2. Pour the mixture into a bowl through a fine mesh strainer.

3. Using a whisk or spoon, force out as much of the deep purple liquid as you can, then set it aside to cool. Discard the blackberry pulp and seeds.

4. Heat the half-and-half and the remaining 1 cup sugar in a saucepan over medium-low heat.

5. Using a whisk, beat the egg yolks until pale yellow and thick.

6. Temper the egg yolks by splashing a very small amount of the warm cream into the yolks, whisking constantly.

7. Pour the tempered yolks into the saucepan . . .

8. Then cook over medium-low heat until thick, stirring constantly, about 5 minutes.

9. Pour the heavy cream into the bowl with the berries . . .

10. Then pour in the custard mixture and stir to combine.

11. Freeze the mixture according to your ice cream maker's instructions.

12. When it's frozen, chop the chocolate into chunks . . .

13. And stir it into the ice cream.

14. Transfer the ice cream to a freezer-safe container and allow it to harden for several hours or overnight.

15. It's ready!

16. And so am I.

17. If you haven't tried this blackberry-and-chocolate combo, my friends, you're missing out on something wonderful.

Moo.

VANILLA BEAN ICE CREAM

Makes 1 quart

Homemade ice cream. Is there anything better in the world? I say there's not, particularly when it's as stripped down and simple as this one. Sugar, cream, eggs, and vanilla. Ahhh . . . it's the simple things in life.

3 cups half-and-half
2 cups sugar

1 vanilla bean
8 large egg yolks

3 cups heavy cream

1. Pour the half-and-half into a saucepan.

2. Add the sugar and stir to combine. Bring the mixture to a simmer over low heat, stirring occasionally.

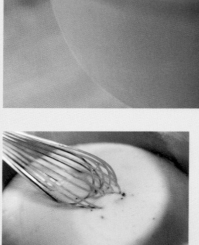

3. Split open the vanilla bean with a small knife, then use the back of the knife to scrape out the "caviar."

4. Throw it into the saucepan . . .

5. Then throw in the bean, too.

6. In a separate bowl, beat the egg yolks until they're light yellow in color.

7. Temper the egg yolks by very slowly drizzling in about 2 cups of the hot half-and-half mixture while whisking quickly.

8. Pour the tempered egg yolk mixture into the saucepan, whisking gently as you add it.

9. Simmer over low heat until it gets very thick, 5 to 7 more minutes.

10. Pour the mixture through a fine-mesh strainer into a medium bowl, pressing with a spoon or spatula to gently force it through.

11. Then pour in the heavy cream.

12. Stir to combine, then cover and refrigerate until cool.

13. Freeze the mixture in your ice cream maker according to the manufacturer's directions, then transfer it to a freezer container. You'll need to freeze the ice cream for a good 12 to 24 hours in order for it to harden and become perfect and wonderful.

14. See? Perfect and wonderful.

It's amazing how that happens.

Variations

- *Serve with Apple Dumplings (page 234), Apple Brown Betty (page 250), Bananas Foster (page 256), or Peach-Basil Ice Cream Topping (page 268).*

- *To create fun varieties, stir in any of the following ingredients after the ice-cream maker stage: chopped semisweet chocolate, chopped peppermint candy, chunks of Oreos, chopped peanut butter cups, chopped toffee, chunks of storebought cookie dough, mashed strawberries, chunks of fresh cherries.*

PEACH-BASIL ICE CREAM TOPPING

Makes 12 servings

Warning: This is a very weird and bizarre topping for ice cream. But the good news is this: You'll love it! Peach and basil are a winning combination, and combining them in a light syrup and spooning them over vanilla ice cream pretty much takes the championship prize.

Oh, and it's purty. And purty covers a multitude of weirdness.

2 cups sugar

18 basil leaves, washed

2 peaches, pitted and chopped

Vanilla Bean Ice Cream (page 266)

1. Combine the sugar and 2 cups water in a medium saucepan and heat over medium heat for 3 to 5 minutes, or until the sugar is fully dissolved. Remove from the heat before it starts to change color. Set aside to cool.

2. Pour into a blender.

3. Add the basil leaves to the syrup in the blender . . .

4. Then pulse it up. You can pulse it just a couple of times to keep some larger chunks of basil, or you can really puree it like I did. Both options are delicious!

5. Place the peaches in a serving bowl and pour the basil syrup over the top.

6. Then just refrigerate the mixture and let the flavors combine for a while.

7. When you're ready, dish up some Vanilla Bean Ice Cream, then spoon the topping over the top.

8. It's sweet and peachy and herby. What more could you ask for?

Pop Quiz: Who loves who more?

COFFEE ICE CREAM

Makes 1 quart

Without a doubt, coffee is my favorite flavor of ice cream. When I eat it, I feel equal parts happy, elated, and naughty. To make my own stash at home, I just use my vanilla bean ice cream recipe, adding a little instant coffee to the custard mixture.

This is the best coffee ice cream you'll ever taste. Consider yourself warned.

**1 recipe Vanilla Bean Ice Cream
(page 266)**

**3 to 4 tablespoons instant coffee
granules**

1. Follow the recipe for Vanilla
Bean Ice Cream through step 8.
Add the coffee granules.

4. Add the heavy cream and stir to
combine. Refrigerate the mixture,
then freeze it according to your
machine's directions.

2. Stir and allow the mixture to
simmer for a few minutes, or until
thick.

5. Transfer it to a freezer
container if you can keep from
eating the whole batch in its soft-
serve stage. Freeze for 12 to 24
hours, or until firm.

3. Pour it into a clean bowl
through a fine-mesh strainer.

6. Serve it up . . . and smile a
million contented smiles. This is
what life's all about.

Variations

- Sandwich Coffee Ice Cream between
  two cookies (page 273).

- Add a variety of chocolate or candy
  toppings to create fun combinations.

- Place in a bowl with a warm
  brownie and drizzle with hot fudge.

My special place.
I drink coffee here.

MALTED MILK CHOCOLATE CHIP COOKIES

Makes about 18 cookies

I've never met a chocolate chip cookie I didn't like. This tastes-like-a-malt version will absolutely rock your world.

1 cup (2 sticks) salted butter, softened

¾ cup packed golden brown granulated sugar

¾ cup granulated sugar

2 eggs

½ cup (rounded) malted milk powder

2 teaspoons vanilla extract

2 cups all-purpose flour

1¼ teaspoons baking soda

1¼ teaspoons salt

One 12-ounce bag milk or semisweet chocolate chips

1. Preheat the oven to 375°F.

2. In a large bowl or your mixer, cream the butter and both sugars until fluffy.

3. Add 1 egg at a time . . .

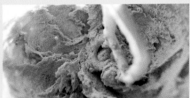

4. Mixing well after each addition.

5. Add the malted milk powder . . .

6. And the vanilla . . .

7. And mix until combined.

8. Sift in the flour, baking soda, and salt.

10. Finally, pour in the chocolate chips and mix until combined.

9. Mix until the ingredients are just incorporated.

11. Using a cookie scoop or spoon, place rounded teaspoons of dough on a cookie sheet lined with a baking mat or wax paper. Leave several inches of space around the cookies since they spread quite a bit.

12. Bake for 10 to 12 minutes, or until dark golden brown. These cookies should be very flat, unlike my abdomen.

Variation
MALTED MILK COFFEE ICE CREAM SANDWICHES

Bad. Very bad. Where *bad* means *awesome*.

Malted Milk Chocolate Chip Cookies (left)

Coffee Ice Cream (page 270), slightly softened

1. When the cookies are cool, take a generous scoop of coffee ice cream . . .

2. And place it on the bottom side of 1 cookie.

3. Press another cookie on the other side. You can enjoy it immediately, or you can wrap it in plastic wrap and freeze it until you need it.

Note: If you like, you can press chocolate sprinkles or mini chocolate chips along the sides of the ice cream.

CANNING

Oh, how I love canning. There's just something about preserving food in mason jars that makes me feel good about life. I love getting the supplies ready, figuring out what kind of fruit I'm going to use to make jam, and deciding whether to put my tomatoes in the smaller jars or the larger ones. I love the signature *pop* of the lids as they seal. And I love the sight of jars of food—food that I've preserved—on the shelves of my pantry. Makes me feel like a pioneer woman.

If you've wanted to jump into canning, there's no easier place to start than jam and pickles. Here are two simple, delicious recipes. Have fun!

Note: When canning food, always follow precise instructions relating to jars, lids, and processing time. There's no place for shortcuts in canning!

STRAWBERRY JAM

Makes twelve 8-ounce jars

I love making jam. Love, love, love making jam. If you want to start canning, it's one of the easiest, most fundamental places to start.

CANNING SUPPLIES

Large canning pot (large enough to submerge the jars in water)

Tongs

Twelve 8-ounce mason jars with lids and screw-on rings

Wide-mouthed canning funnel

Canning rack to go inside the pot

STRAWBERRY JAM

7½ cups mashed strawberries (approximately 5 pints)

6 tablespoons fresh lemon juice, strained

One and a half 49-gram packages fruit pectin

10½ cups sugar

1. First, fill the canning pot two-thirds full of water and bring it to a simmer. Using tongs, submerge the jars in the water. Leave them there with the water simmering while you prepare the jam. This is to temper the jars and prepare them for the hot jelly.

2. Meanwhile, bring a small saucepan of water to a simmer and add the jar lids (but not the screw-on rings). Allow them to stay in the saucepan while you prepare the jam.

3. Place the hulled strawberries on a large baking sheet and mash them . . .

4. Until they're mostly mashed but still have large chunks in them.

5. Measure out 7½ cups of strawberries . . .

6. And throw them into a pot.

7. Add the lemon juice . . .

8. And give them a stir.

9. Bring the strawberries to a boil over high heat . . .

10. Then pour in the powdered pectin and stir it to combine.

11. After that, pour in the sugar all at once.

12. Stir it around and bring it to a hard boil, which means you can't get it to stop boiling when you stir it down.

13. Allow to remain at a hard boil for 1 minute and 25 seconds. Turn off the heat, then skim off and discard the excess foam from the top of the mixture.

14. One at a time, remove the jars from the hot water.

15. Place each jar on the countertop and insert the mouth of a wide-mouthed canning funnel.

16. Using a metal measuring cup or ladle, pour the preserves through the funnel into the jar.

17. Stop when the jam is ¼ inch from the top of the jar.

18. Use a damp cloth to wipe off any stickiness from the jar.

19. Then run a knife along the inside of the jar to remove any air pockets.

20. Remove one of the lids from the simmering water and set it on top of the jar.

21. Center it, then screw the round ring on the outside of the jar. Don't overtighten the lids; just attach them gently.

22. Continue until they're all filled.

23. Next, turn up the heat on the pot of water to high. When the water is boiling, set all the jars into the rack . . .

24. And lower the rack to submerge the jars in water. Cover the pot and allow it to boil for 15 minutes. Turn off the heat and leave the jars in the water for 15 minutes more.

25. Lift the rack from the water and remove the jars. Allow them to sit on the counter undisturbed for 24 hours; over a period of time, you should hear the lids pop as they seal themselves. It's a very satisfying sound!

26. After 24 hours, check the seals of all the jars: Remove the rings from the jars and press your finger in the center of each jar. The center of the lids should be tightly indented and not give at all when you press your finger on them. If any jars failed to seal, just store the jam in the fridge.

Store the jam in the pantry . . . or give it to your friends! Refrigerate the jam once the jars are opened.

Munchin'. At the cowboy luncheon.

SWEET LIME PICKLES

Makes about 8 pint jars

Marlboro Man's grandmother Edna Mae makes sweet lime pickles, and they're the best pickles I've ever tasted. Exceptional on sandwiches or burgers, they're also pretty much a snack in themselves. Crunchy, sweet, flavorful, and spicy, and they make a great homemade gift.

Canning supplies (page 276)

16 to 20 small/medium cucumbers (about 5 pounds) (pickling cucumbers are preferred, but standard cucumbers are fine!)

1 cup pickling lime (sold in the canning aisle)

8 cups white distilled vinegar

8 cups sugar

2 tablespoons pickling spices

1 teaspoon turmeric

1 teaspoon salt

½ teaspoon cayenne pepper

1. Lop off the tops and bottoms of the cucumbers . . .

4. Then grab some pickling lime.

7. Cover the pot and refrigerate the cucumbers for several hours or overnight. This'll help the pickles become really, really crisp.

2. And cut them into ½-inch-thick slices.

5. Mix it with 8 cups of water . . .

8. Rinse the cucumbers in cold water 3 times in order to remove the lime solution thoroughly. If you'll be using the same pot to make the pickles, thoroughly clean/rinse the pot before adding the cucumbers back in.

3. Throw them into a very large pot . . .

6. And pour it into the pot with the cucumbers.

9. To the pot of cucumbers, add the vinegar . . .

11. Pickling spices . . .

13. Bring the mixture almost to a boil, then turn off the heat, stir, and cover the pot. Place in the fridge for another 3 to 4 hours.

10. Sugar . . .

12. Turmeric, salt, and cayenne.

14. Pull the pickles out of the fridge and boil them over medium-high heat on the stovetop for 40 to 45 minutes, stirring occasionally.

"Pardon me. Do you have any Grey Poupon?"

15. In a separate pot, heat 8 pint mason jars and lids using the method on page 276.

16. One at a time, remove a jar from the hot water and place a wide-mouthed funnel inside the jar. Fill it with pickle slices.

17. When you've gotten as many pickles in the jar as you can, pour in enough liquid to reach ¼ inch from the top of the jar.

18. Place the lid on the jar and repeat with the rest of the pickles. Place the jars in the canner and heat process for 15 to 20 minutes. Remove them from the boiling water and allow them to sit on the countertop for 24 hours. After that time, check to make sure the lids are completely sealed; if any jars failed to seal, just store the pickles in the fridge.

If you can make sweet lime pickles, you can do most anything in life!

Variations

Add to Basic Chicken Salad (page 50), His/Her Burgers (page 160), or Drip Beef (page 64).

"Pardon me. What's Grey Poupon?"

KEEPIN' IT REAL

Someday I'm going to write a book about writing a cookbook.

It'll be in the suspense/thriller/horror genre, filled with more mystery and tragedy than most epic novels out there.

I want my mommy.

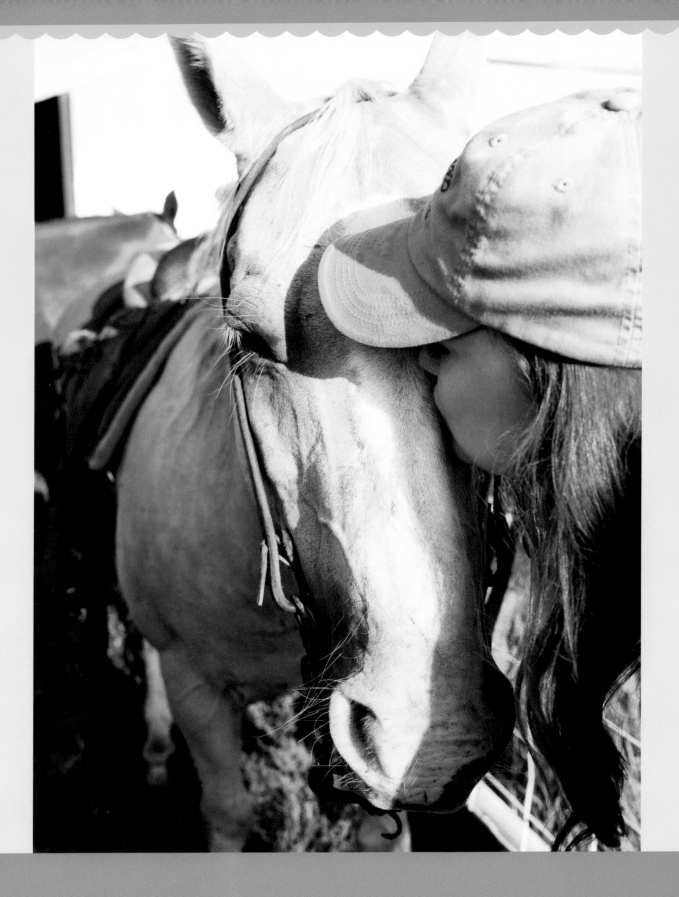

ACKNOWLEDGMENTS

To the beautiful, kind, and wonderful folks who stop by and read my website, The Pioneer Woman. Many of you have been there from the beginning and I love and appreciate you all so very much. Thank you for your unending love and support.

To the precious blogging friends I've met through the years. There are just too many of you to name . . . but you know who you are. I'm so glad this strange little medium brought us all together.

To all the talented contributors and members of Tasty Kitchen. You're the best of the best, the cream of the crop, and I'm so honored to have you as part of the community.

To Tiffany Poe, for your tremendous hands-on help, support, and friendship. Without our mutual friend Hyacinth, I wouldn't have finished my first cookbook. Without you, there's no way I would have finished this one. Obi Wan and Yoda forever!

To Hyacinth. You're my touchstone, Emma.

To my editor and friend, Cassie Jones Morgan. I still don't know what I did to deserve you. Never leave me.

To Jessica McGrady, Sharyn Rosenblum, Susanna Einstein, and Kassie Evashevski, for your hard work, support, and friendship.

To my forever friends, Beccus, Jenn, Connell, Jules, Sarah, Moosh, Carrie, Ang, Christy, Shelley, Susan, Kash, Kristie, Katy, Amy, and Shane. See you in July!

To my mom, Gerre, for your delicious cooking and your lifelong example of joy.

To my sister, Betsy, for being the most perfect sister in the history of man. (I mean woman.)

To my in-laws, Chuck and Nan, for always loving me like I'm your own daughter.

To Tim Kill, Pete Mauricio, Chris Potter, Todd Armstrong, and Josh Sellers, for your dedication.

To my dad, Bill, for your selfless love and support.

To my children, for being smart and sweet and funny and weird and everything I could ever ask for. Mama loves you forever.

To Tim, Missy, Halle, Caleb, Mike, Doug, Nic, Stuart, Matt, Reagan, Elliot, Patsy, Doug, Edna Mae, Lindy, Morgan, Julie, Butch, Capie, Ken, Alice, Elise, Jaden, Erika, Nanci, Sean, and Nick. Thank you for everything. Love you guys.

And to my husband, for being my best friend. And for your Wranglers. And for your chaps.

(I'll stop now.)

Say wha?

INDEX

A

Almonds
    Basic Chicken Salad, 50–51
Appetizers and starters
    Asian Hot Wings, 108–9
    Brie-Stuffed Mushrooms, 96–97
    Caprese Salad, 98–99
    Classic Hot Wings, 106–7
    Fried Mozzarella, 104–5
    Grilled Corn Guacamole, 90–91
    Hummus, 94–95
    Meatball Sliders, 103
    Mushroom Swiss Sliders with Spicy
        Fry Sauce, 100–102
    Restaurant-Style Salsa, 92–93
    Whiskey-Mustard Meatballs, 112–13
Apple(s)
    Brown Betty, 250–51
    Dumplings, 234–35
    and Grits, Pork Chops with, 200–203
Apricot
    Chicken Panini, 56–57
    -Shrimp Skewers, 183–85
Arugula
    Fig-Prosciutto Pizza, 148–49
Asian Hot Wings, 108–9
Avocados
    Grilled Corn Guacamole, 90–91

B

Bacon
    Breakfast Pizza, 26–27
    Cowboy Quiche, 32–33
    Fancy Mac and Cheese, 132–35
    Green Bean Casserole, 218–19
    His/Her Burgers, 160–61
    Make-Ahead Muffin Melts, 12–13
    Perfect Spinach Salad, 60–61
    Pork Chops with Apples and Grits,
        200–203
    Ranch-Style Chicken, 208–9
Bacon, Canadian
    Eggs Benedict, 17–18
Bananas Foster, 256–57
Barbecue Chicken and Pineapple
    Quesadillas, 154–55

Basil
    Caprese Salad, 98–99
    Pasta with Pesto Cream Sauce,
        136–38
    -Peach Ice Cream Topping, 268–69
Bean(s)
    and Beef Burritos, 66–67
    Chicken Tortilla Soup, 76–78
    Green, Casserole, 218–19
    Hummus, 94–95
Bean sprouts
    Thai Chicken Pizza, 145–47
Beef. *See also* Veal
    and Bean Burritos, 66–67
    Carnitas Pizza, 150–51
    Chipotle Steak Salad, 48–49
    Drip, 64–65
    His/Her Burgers, 160–61
    Italian Meatball Soup, 79–81
    Meatball Sliders, 103
    Mushroom Swiss Sliders with Spicy
        Fry Sauce, 100–102
    Noodle Salad, Sesame, 63
    Rib-Eye Steak with Onion–Blue
        Cheese Sauce, 204–5
    Rigatoni and Meatballs, 126–29
    Shepherd's Pie, 168–69
    Sloppy Joes, 58–59
    Steakhouse Pizza, 142–44
    Stew, 165–67
    Tangy Tomato Brisket, 180–81
    Whiskey-Mustard Meatballs, 112–13
Berry(ies)
    Blackberry Chip Ice Cream, 263–65
    Butter, French Toast with, 28–30
    Lemon Blueberry Pancakes, 22–23
    Strawberry Jam, 276–79
    Strawberry Shortcake Cake, 246–49
Blackberry(ies)
    Chip Ice Cream, 263–65
    French Toast with Berry Butter,
        28–30
Bloody Mary, 118–19
Blueberry Pancakes, Lemon, 22–23
Blue Cheese
    Dip, 106–7
    Fancy Mac and Cheese, 132–35
    His/Her Burgers, 160–61

    –Onion Sauce, Rib-Eye Steak with,
        204–5
Bread(s). *See also* Tortilla(s)
    Buttered Rosemary Rolls, 228–29
    Cornbread Croutons, 42
    French Toast with Berry Butter,
        28–30
    Orange Sweet Rolls, 14–16
    Pudding, Breakfast, 24–25
Breakfast
    Breakfast Bread Pudding, 24–25
    Breakfast Pizza, 26–27
    Cowboy Quiche, 32–33
    Cowgirl Quiche, 34–36
    Eggs Benedict, 17–18
    Eggs Florentine, 19
    French Toast with Berry Butter,
        28–30
    Homemade Glazed Doughnuts,
        8–11
    Lemon Blueberry Pancakes, 22–23
    Make-Ahead Muffin Melts, 12–13
    Orange Sweet Rolls, 14–16
    Perfect Iced Coffee, 6–7
Brie-Stuffed Mushrooms, 96–97
Brownies, Knock You Naked, 260–62
Burgers
    His/Her, 160–61
    Meatball Sliders, 103
    Mushroom Swiss Sliders with Spicy
        Fry Sauce, 100–102
Burritos, Beef and Bean, 66–67
Butter, Berry, French Toast with, 28–30

C

Caesar Salad, Spicy, 40–41
Cakes
    Billie's Italian Cream, 241–43
    Coffee Cream, 252–55
    Strawberry Shortcake, 246–49
    Tres Leches, 238–40
Canadian bacon
    Eggs Benedict, 17–18
Caprese Salad, 98–99
Carnitas Pizza, 150–51
Carrots
    Beef Stew, 165–67

Doughnuts, Homemade Glazed, 8–11
Drinks
    Bloody Mary, 118–19
    Cherry Limeade, 114–15
    Dulce de Leche Coffee, 232–33
    Mango Margaritas, 116–17
    Perfect Iced Coffee, 6–7
    Watermelon Granita, 120–23
Dr Pepper Pulled Pork, Spicy,
    158–59
Dulce de Leche Coffee, 232–33
Dumplings, Apple, 234–35

E

Eggs
    Benedict, 17–18
    Breakfast Pizza, 26–27
    Florentine, 19
    Make-Ahead Muffin Melts, 12–13
    Perfect Spinach Salad, 60–61
Enchiladas, White Chicken, 186–89
English muffins
    Eggs Benedict, 17–18
    Eggs Florentine, 19
    Make-Ahead Muffin Melts,
        12–13

F

Fig-Prosciutto Pizza, 148–49
French Onion Soup, 84–85
French Toast with Berry Butter, 28–30

G

Garlic
    Lemon Shrimp, Spicy, 206–7
    Panfried Kale, 214–15
    Panfried Spinach, 216
Gazpacho, 70–72
Grains
    Cornbread Croutons, 42
    Mexican Rice, 173
    Pork Chops with Apples and Grits,
        200–203
    Risotto, 194–96
Granita, Watermelon, 120–23
Grapes
    Basic Chicken Salad, 50–51
Green Bean Casserole, 218–19
Greens. *See also* Spinach
    Chipotle Steak Salad, 48–49
    Fig-Prosciutto Pizza, 148–49

Panfried Kale, 214–15
    Spicy Caesar Salad, 40–41
Grits and Apples, Pork Chops with,
    200–203
Gruyère cheese
    Fancy Mac and Cheese, 132–35
    French Onion Soup, 84–85
Guacamole, Grilled Corn, 90–91

H

Ham
    Cowgirl Quiche, 34–36
    Fig-Prosciutto Pizza, 148–49
Herb-Roasted Pork Tenderloin, 190–93
Honey-Plum-Soy Chicken, 197–99
Hummus, 94–95

I

Ice Cream
    Blackberry Chip, 263–65
    Coffee, 270–71
    Sandwiches, Coffee Malted Milk, 273
    Topping, Peach-Basil, 268–69
    Vanilla Bean, 266–67
Italian Meatball Soup, 79–81

J

Jam, Strawberry, 276–79

K

Kale, Panfried, 214–15

L

Lemon
    Blueberry Pancakes, 22–23
    Citrus Butter Cookies, 236–37
    Garlic Shrimp, Spicy, 206–7
Lime(s)
    Cherry Limeade, 114–15
    Citrus Butter Cookies, 236–37
    Mango Margaritas, 116–17
    Tequila Chicken, 170–72
    Watermelon Granita, 120–23
Lunch
    Basic Chicken Salad, 50–51
    Beef and Bean Burritos, 66–67
    Best Grilled Cheese Ever, 43–45
    Chicken Apricot Panini, 56–57
    Chipotle Steak Salad, 48–49

Curried Chicken Pasta Salad, 52
Drip Beef, 64–65
Perfect Spinach Salad, 60–61
Sesame Beef Noodle Salad, 63
Simple Sesame Noodles, 62–63
Sloppy Joes, 58–59
Spicy Caesar Salad, 40–41
Spicy Grilled Vegetable Panini, 53–55

M

Mac and Cheese, Fancy, 132–35
Malted Milk Chocolate Chip Cookies,
    272–73
Malted Milk Coffee Ice Cream
    Sandwiches, 273
Mango Margaritas, 116–17
Margaritas, Mango, 116–17
Meatball(s)
    Rigatoni and, 126–29
    Sliders, 103
    Soup, Italian, 79–81
    Whiskey-Mustard, 112–13
Mexican Rice, 173
Monterey Jack cheese
    Barbecue Chicken and Pineapple
        Quesadillas, 154–55
    Breakfast Bread Pudding, 24–25
    Pork Chops with Apples and Grits,
        200–203
    Quesadillas de Camarones, 156–57
    Twice-Baked New Potatoes, 212–13
    White Chicken Enchiladas, 186–89
Mozzarella
    Breakfast Pizza, 26–27
    Caprese Salad, 98–99
    Carnitas Pizza, 150–51
    Fig-Prosciutto Pizza, 148–49
    Fried, 104–5
    Meatball Sliders, 103
    Steakhouse Pizza, 142–44
    Thai Chicken Pizza, 145–47
Muffin Melts, Make-Ahead, 12–13
Mushroom(s)
    Brie-Stuffed, 96–97
    Cowgirl Quiche, 34–36
    Fancy Mac and Cheese, 132–35
    His/Her Burgers, 160–61
    Perfect Spinach Salad, 60–61
    Risotto, 194–96
    Spicy Grilled Vegetable Panini,
        53–55
    Swiss Sliders with Spicy Fry Sauce,
        100–102

The End